Trucks Planes And Cars Coloring Book

Fun Vehicle Coloring Book Designed Especially For Kids of All Ages

SUNNY HAPPY KIDS

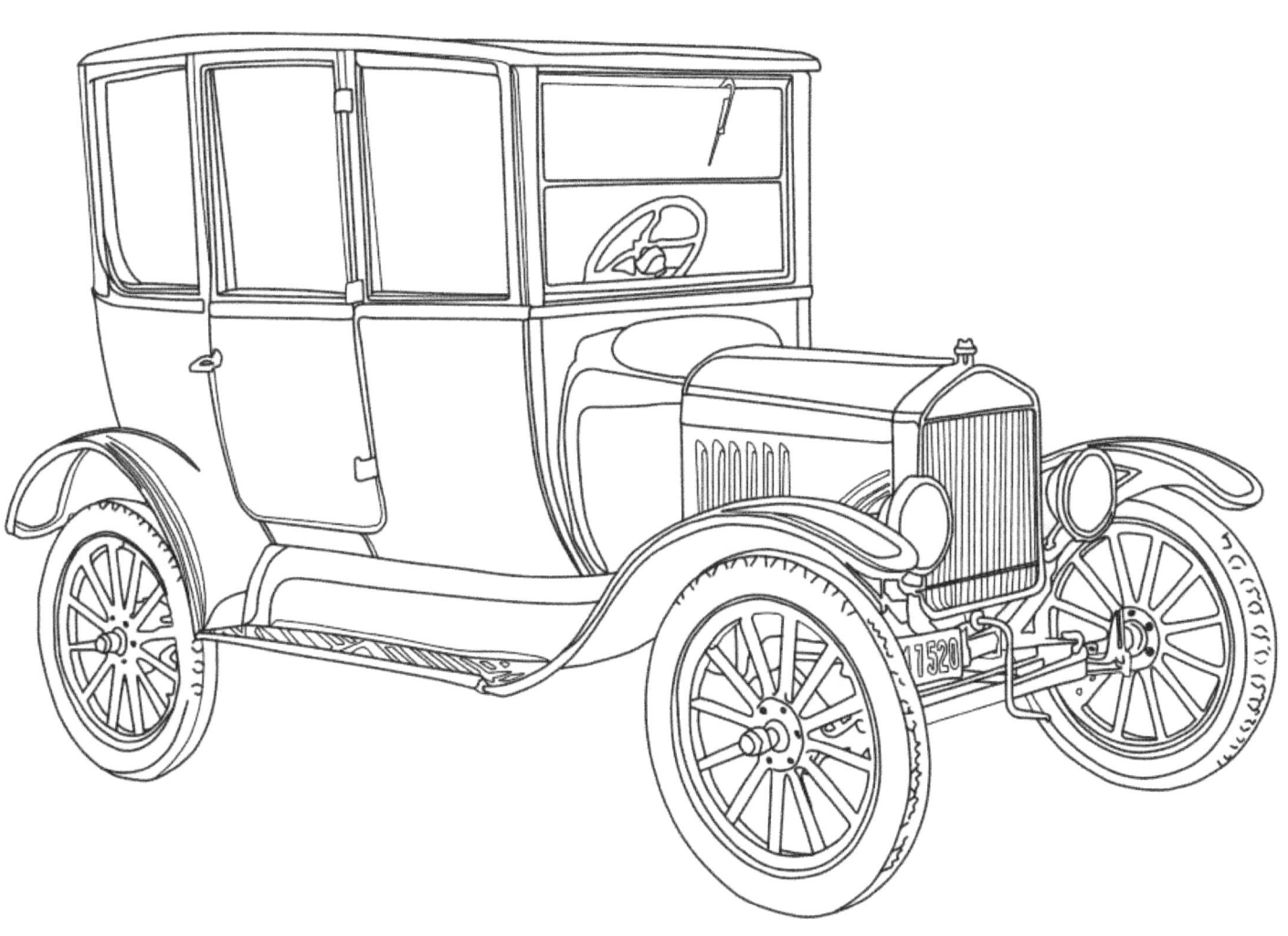

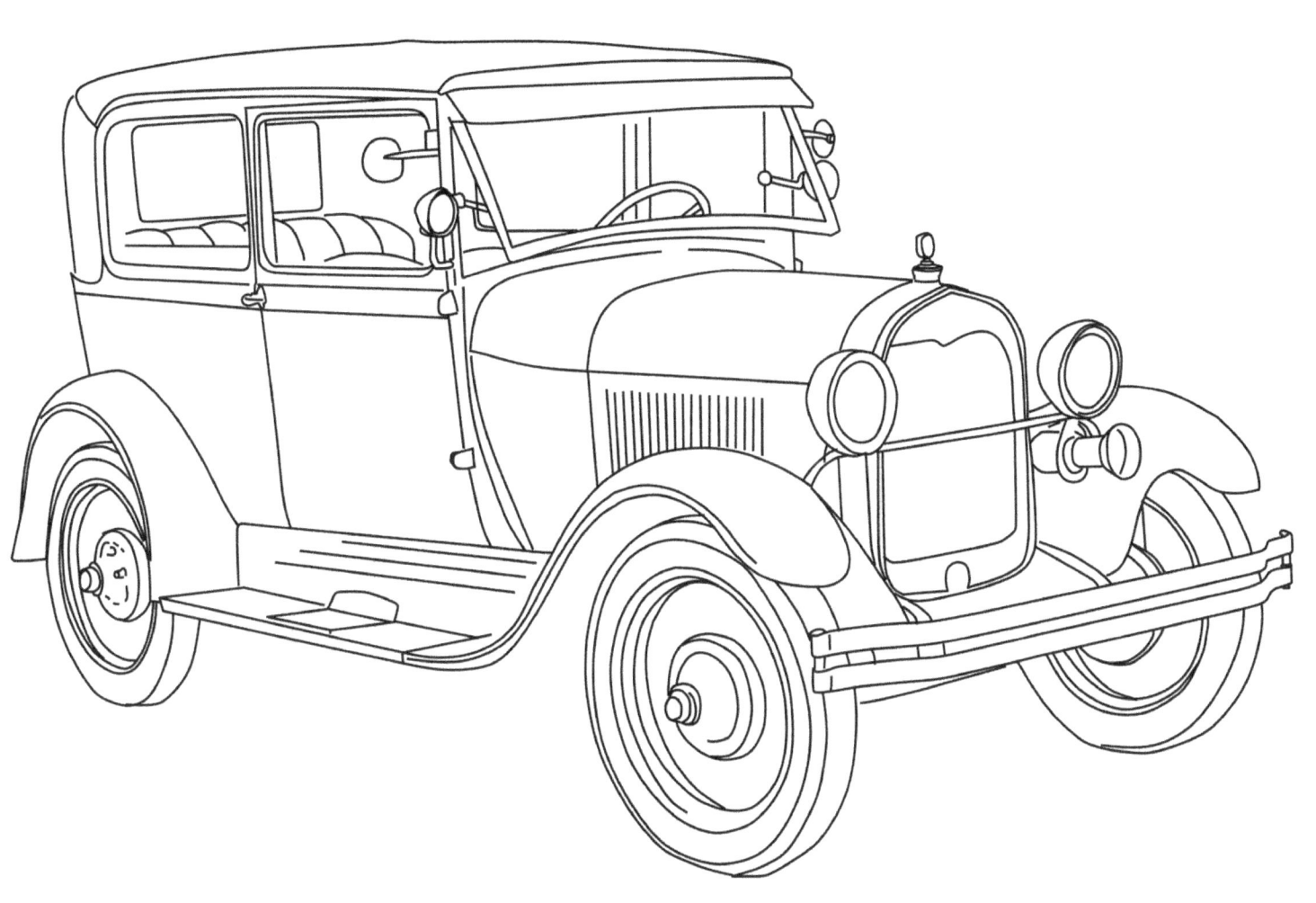

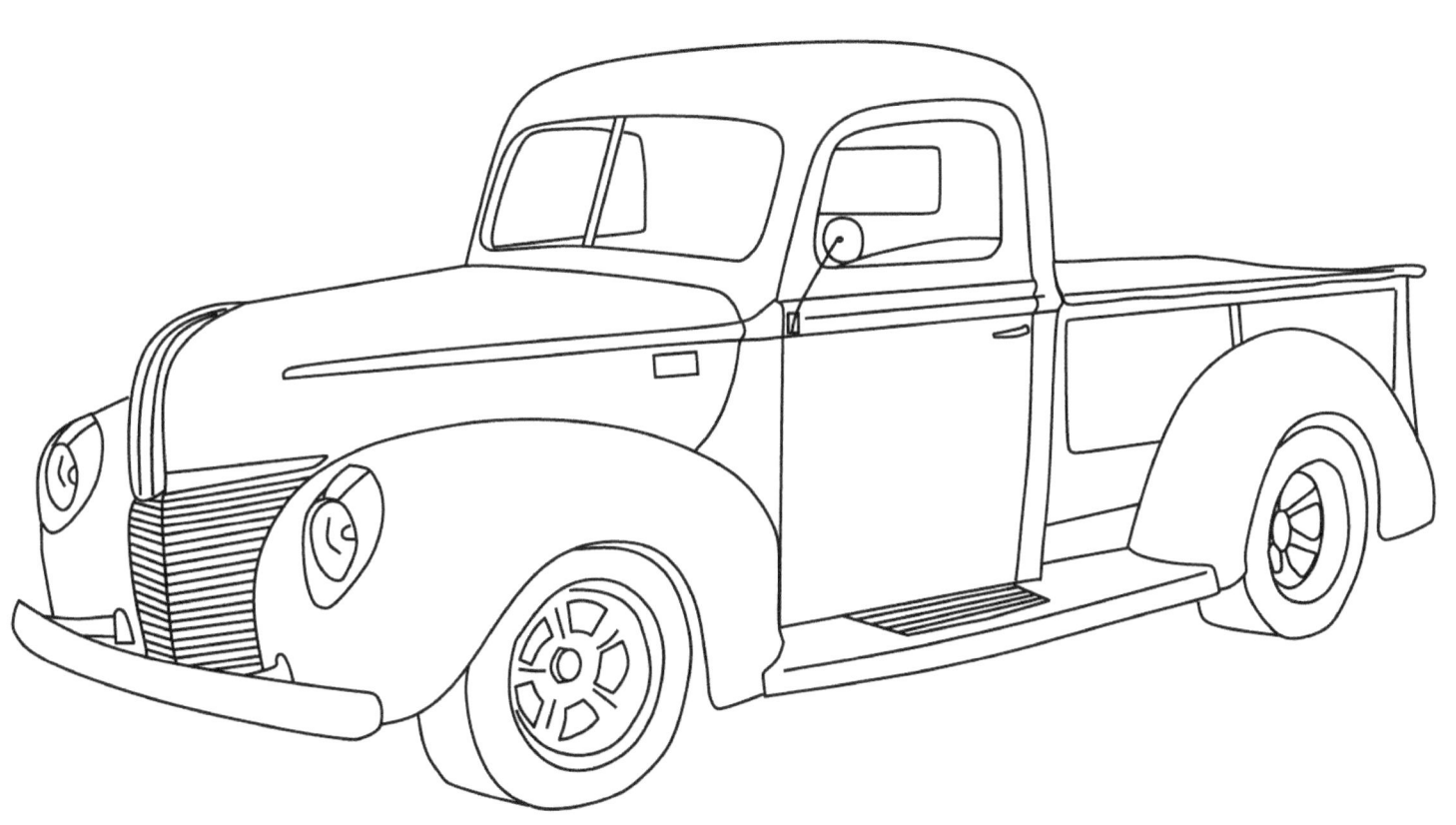

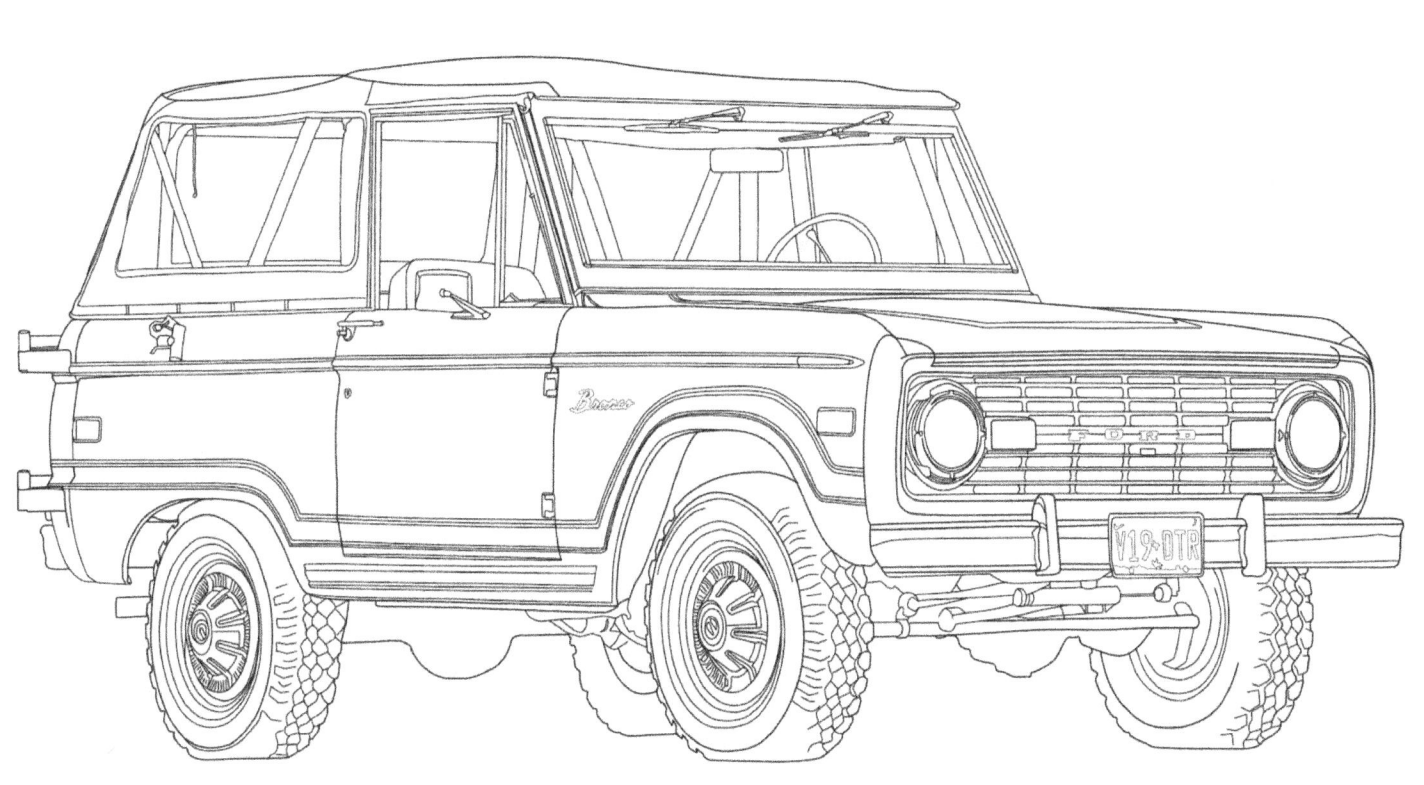

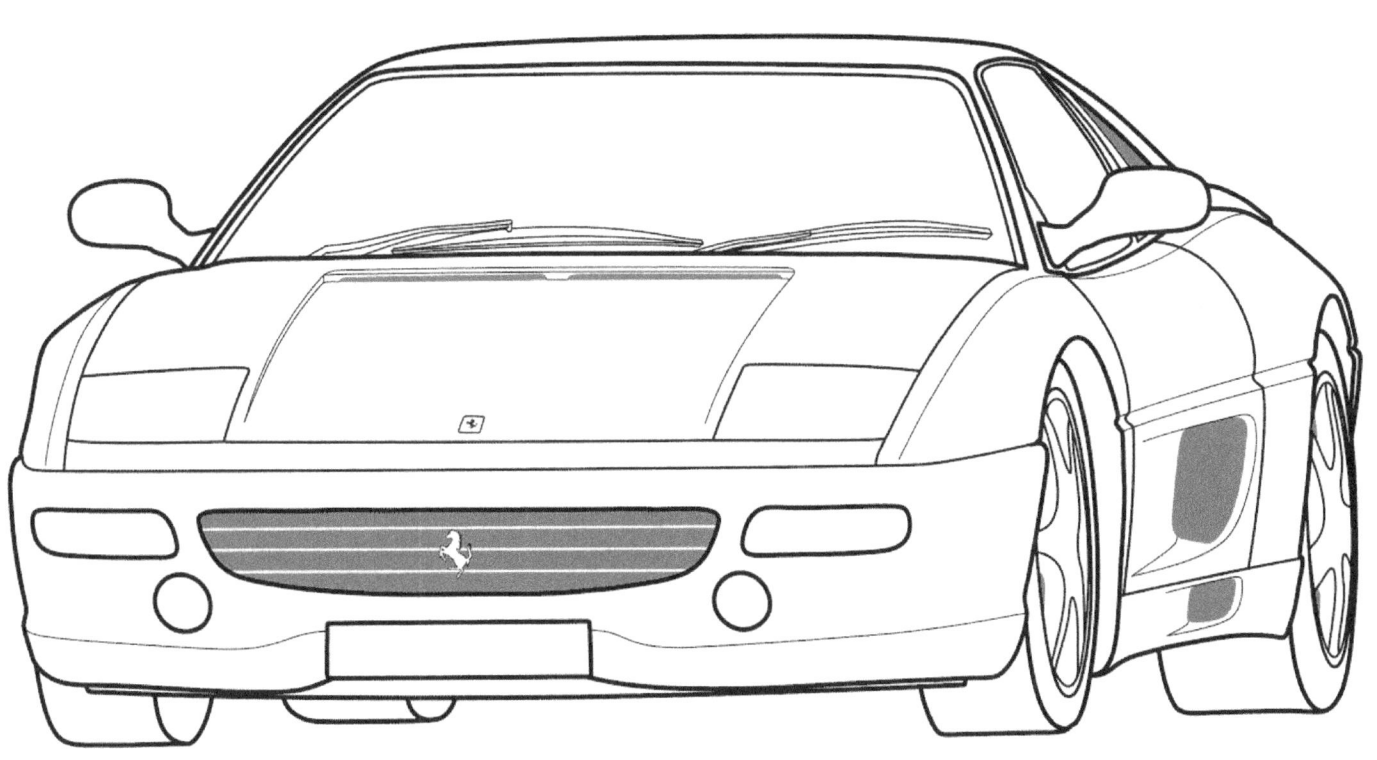

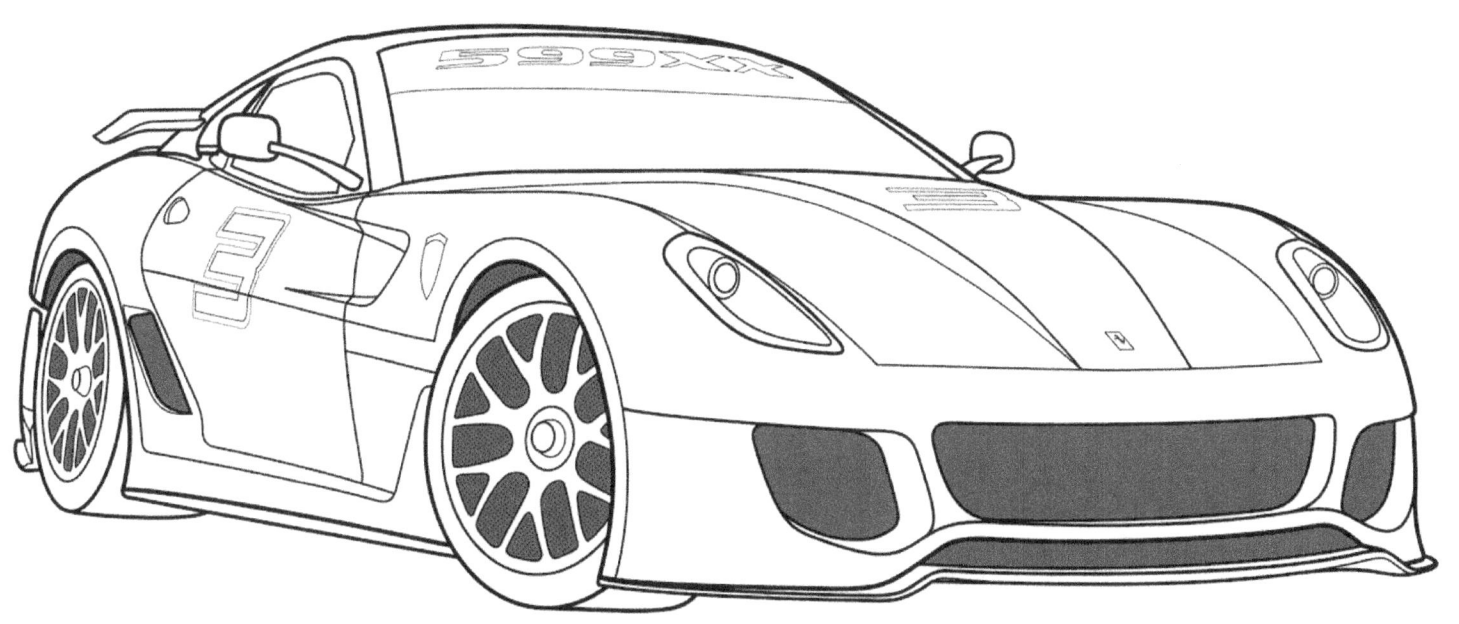

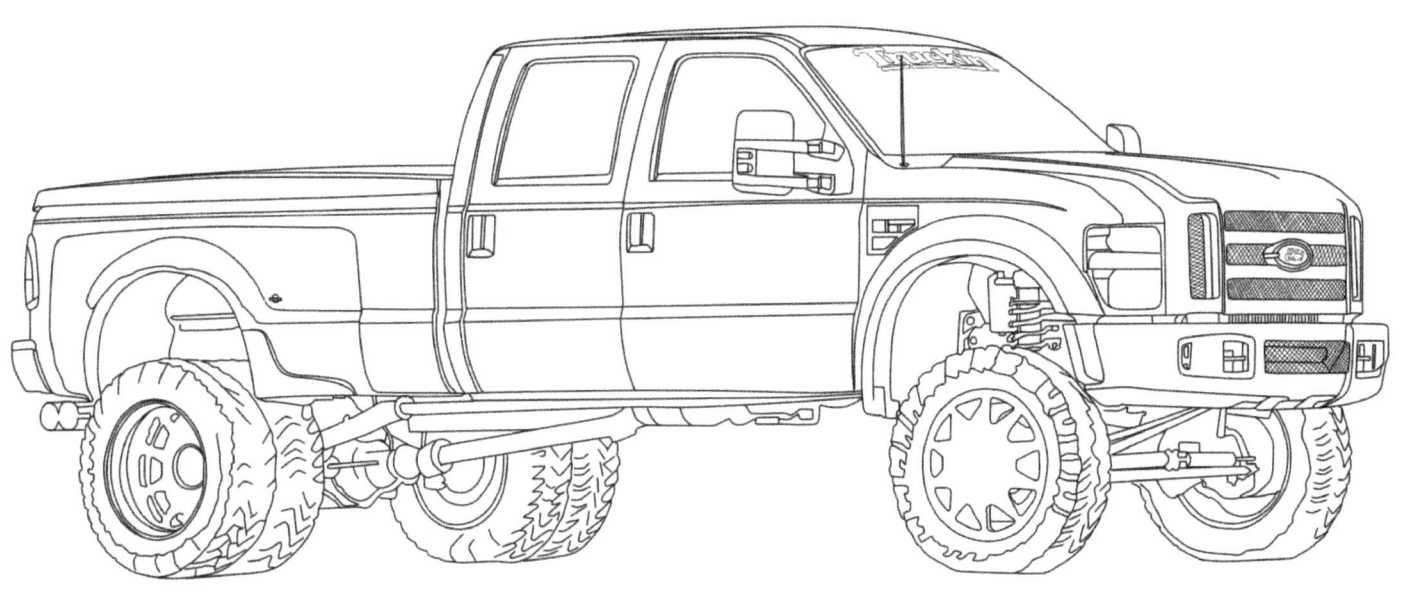

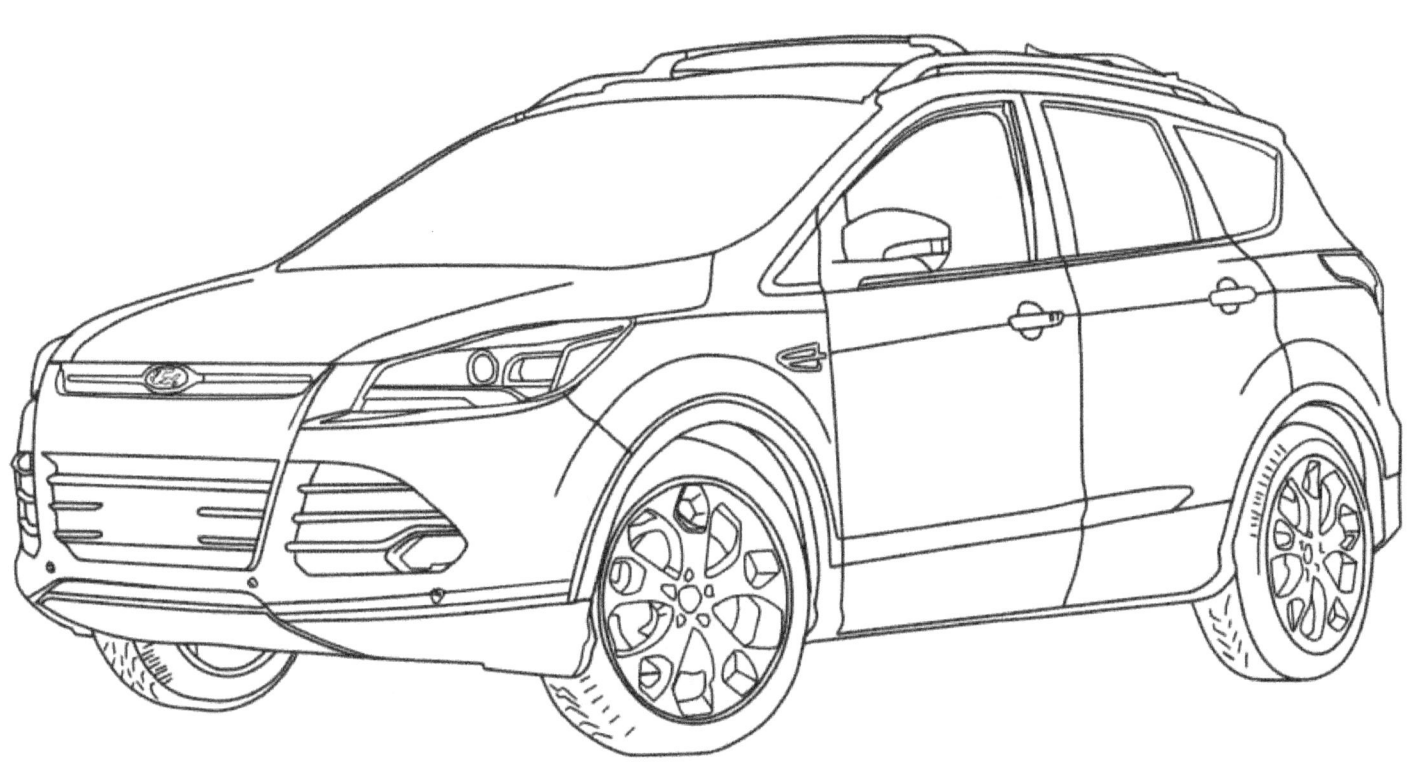

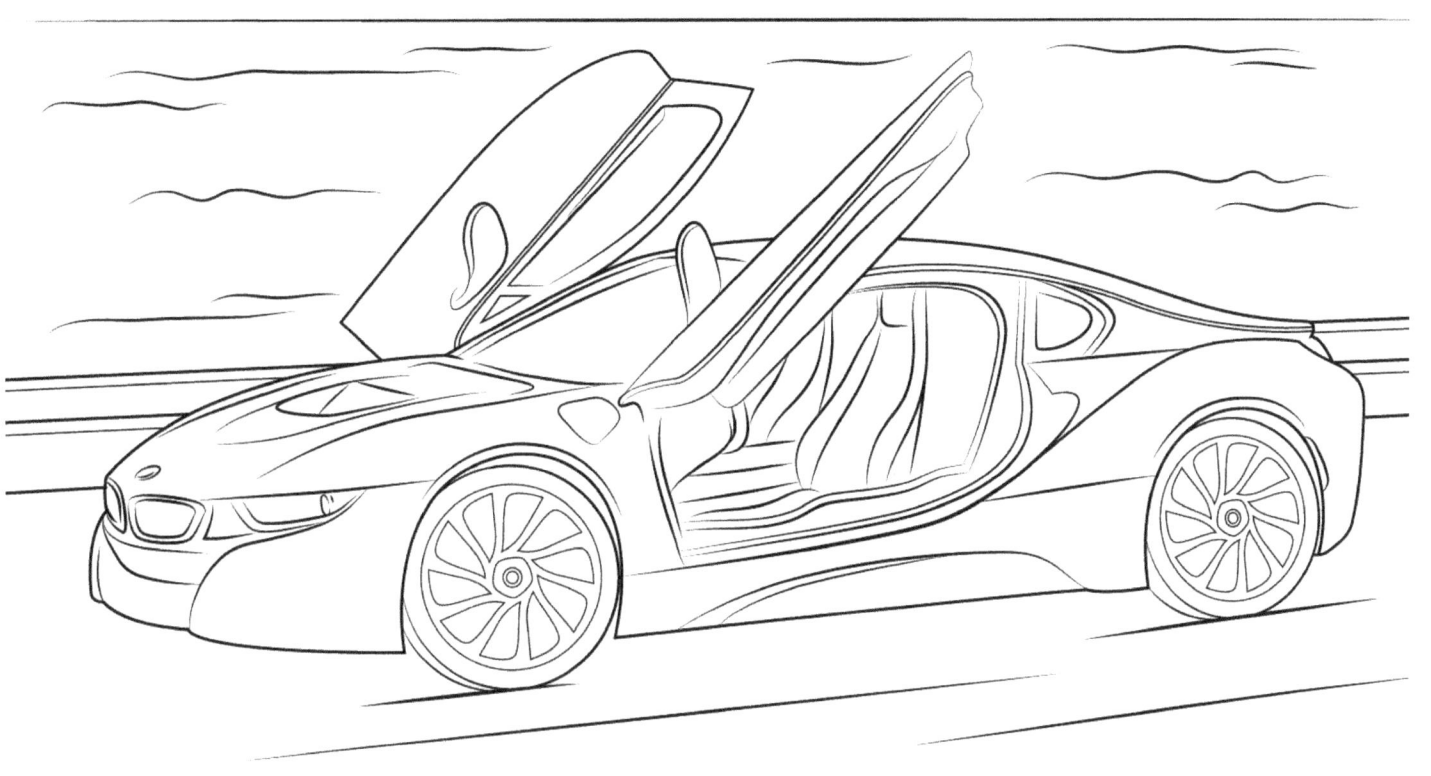

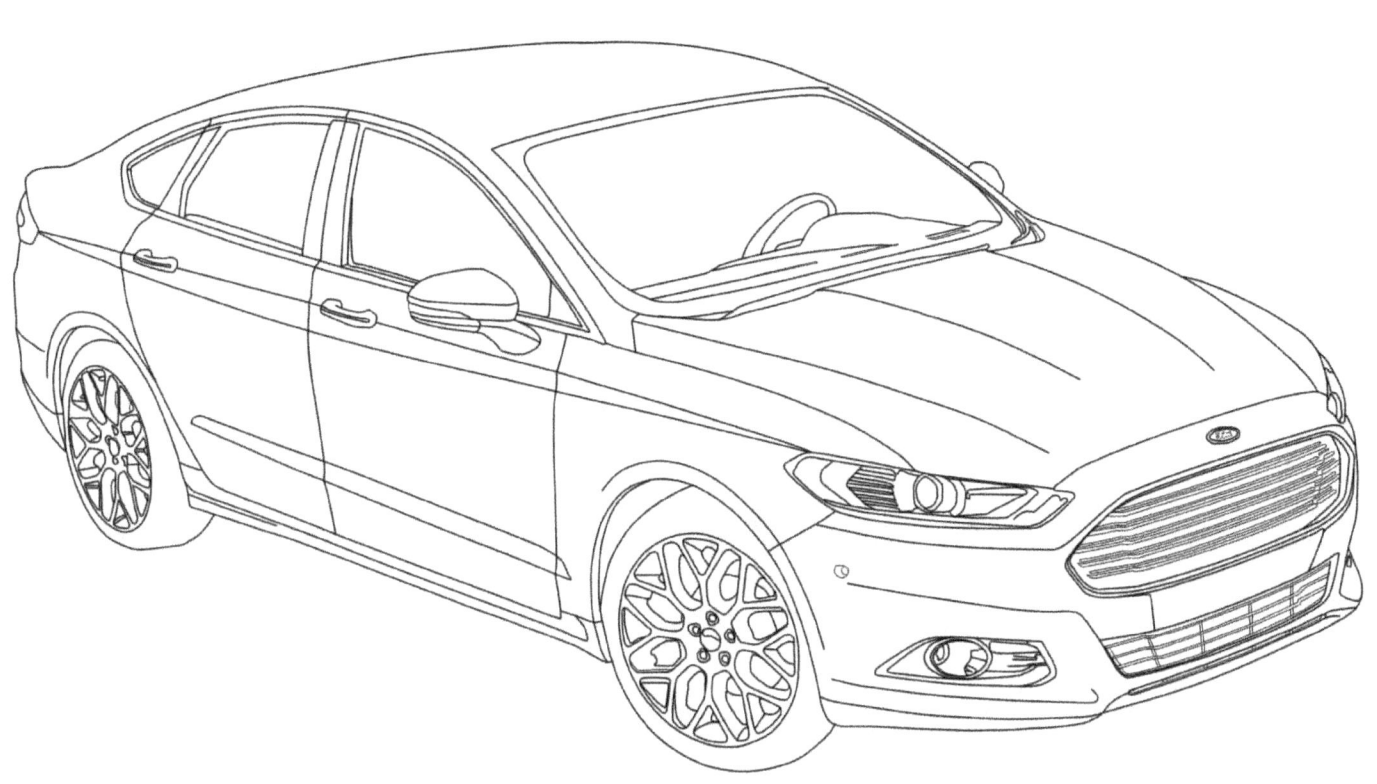

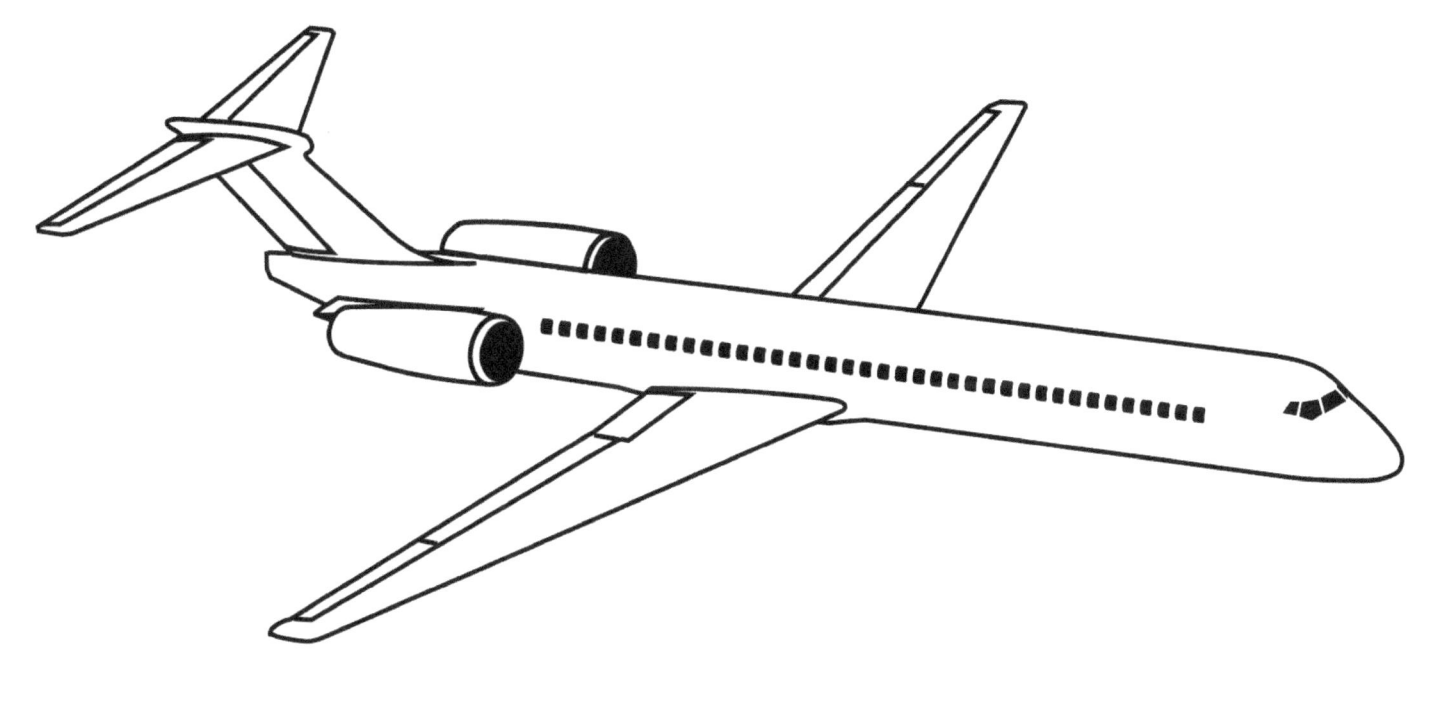

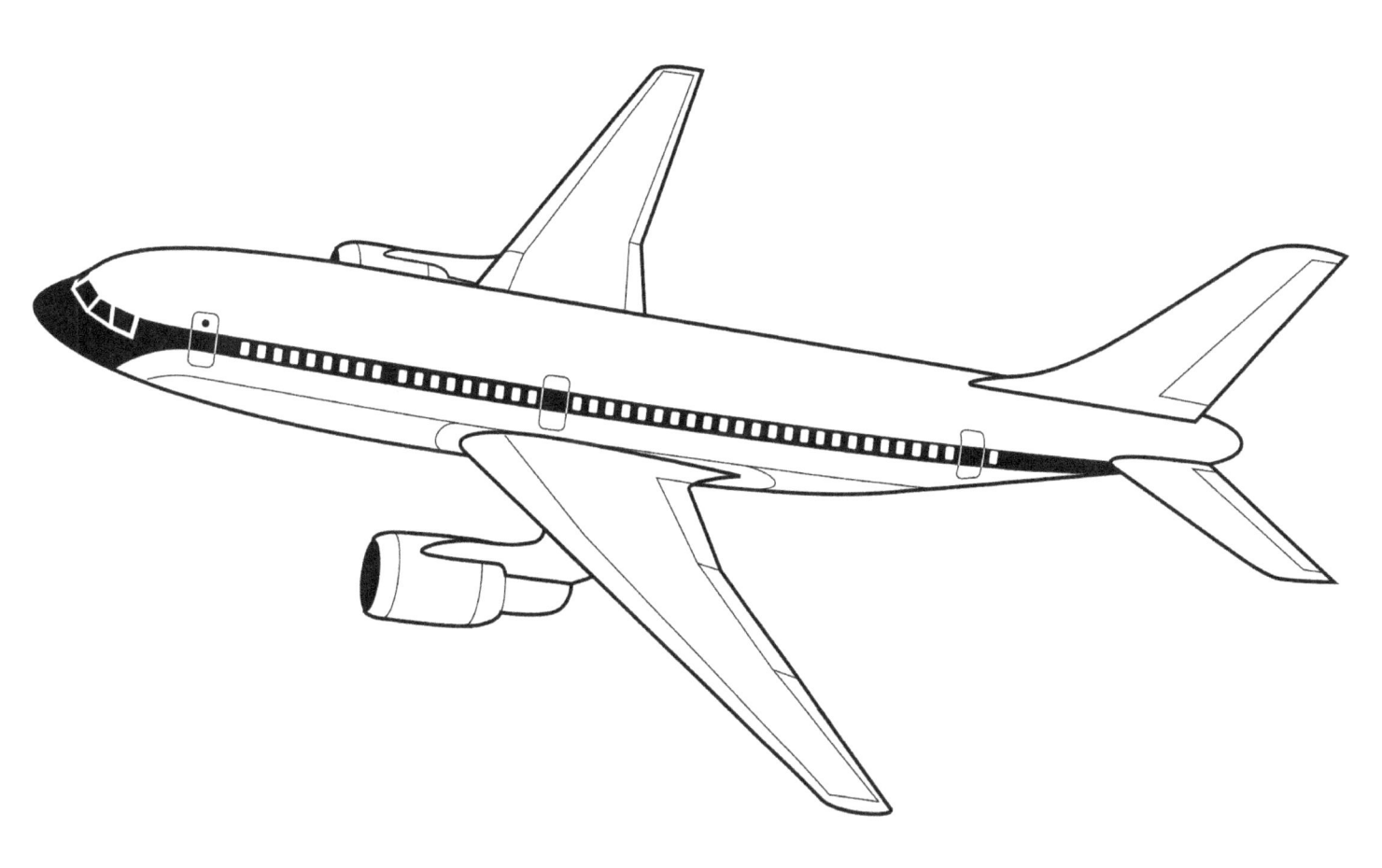

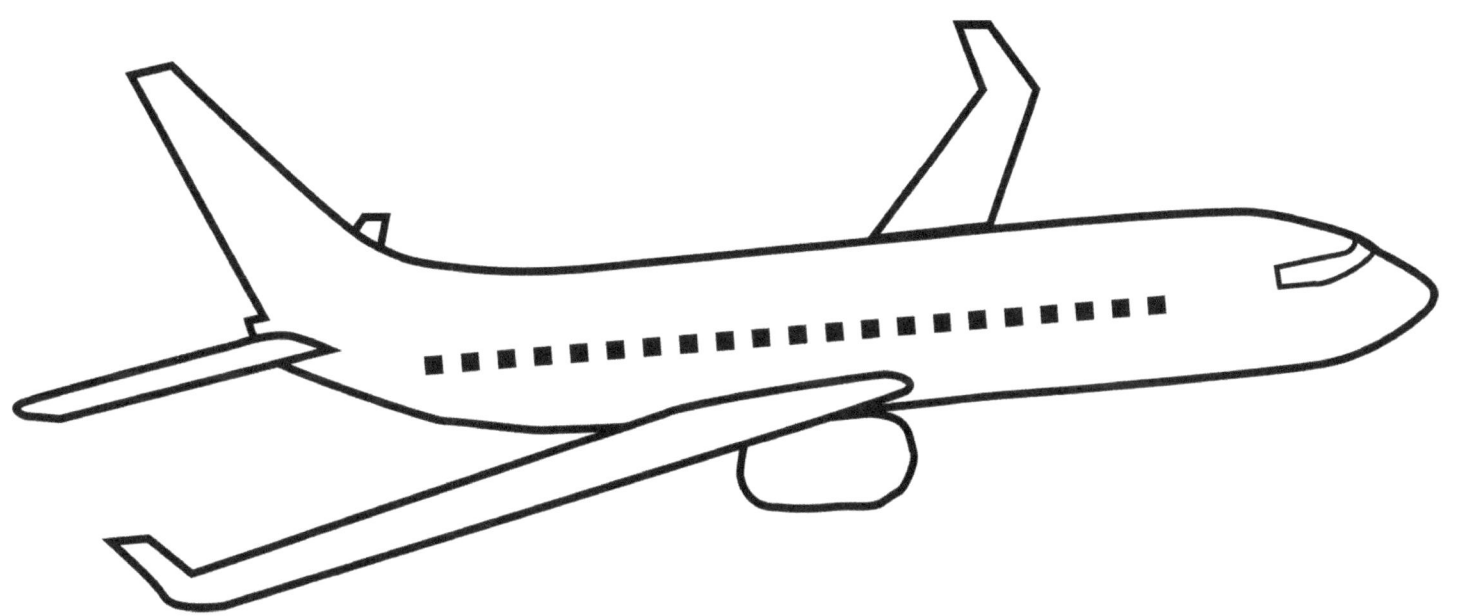

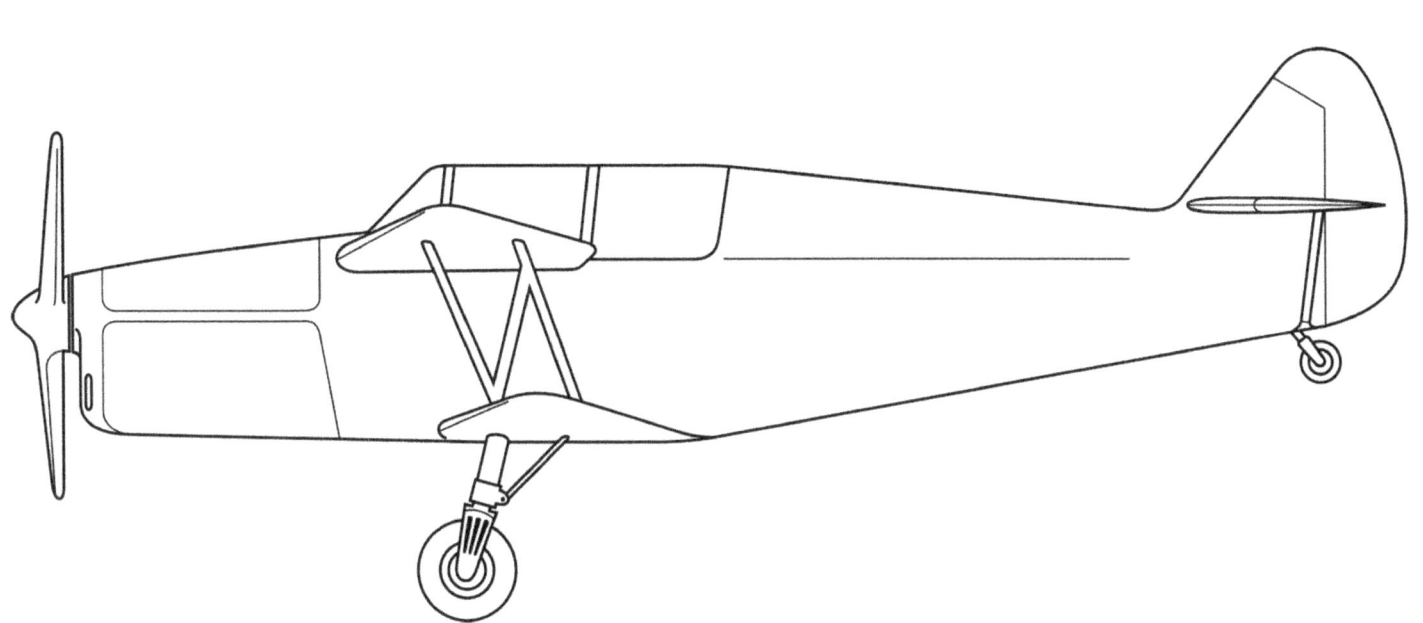

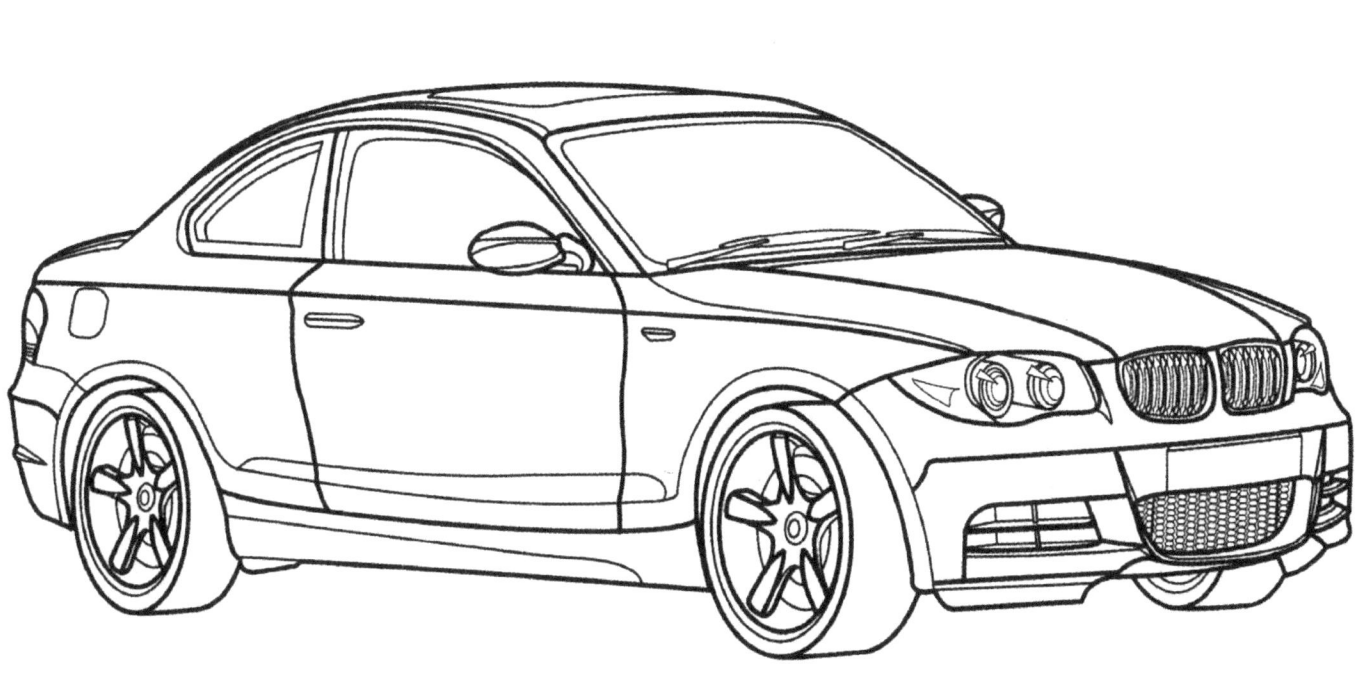

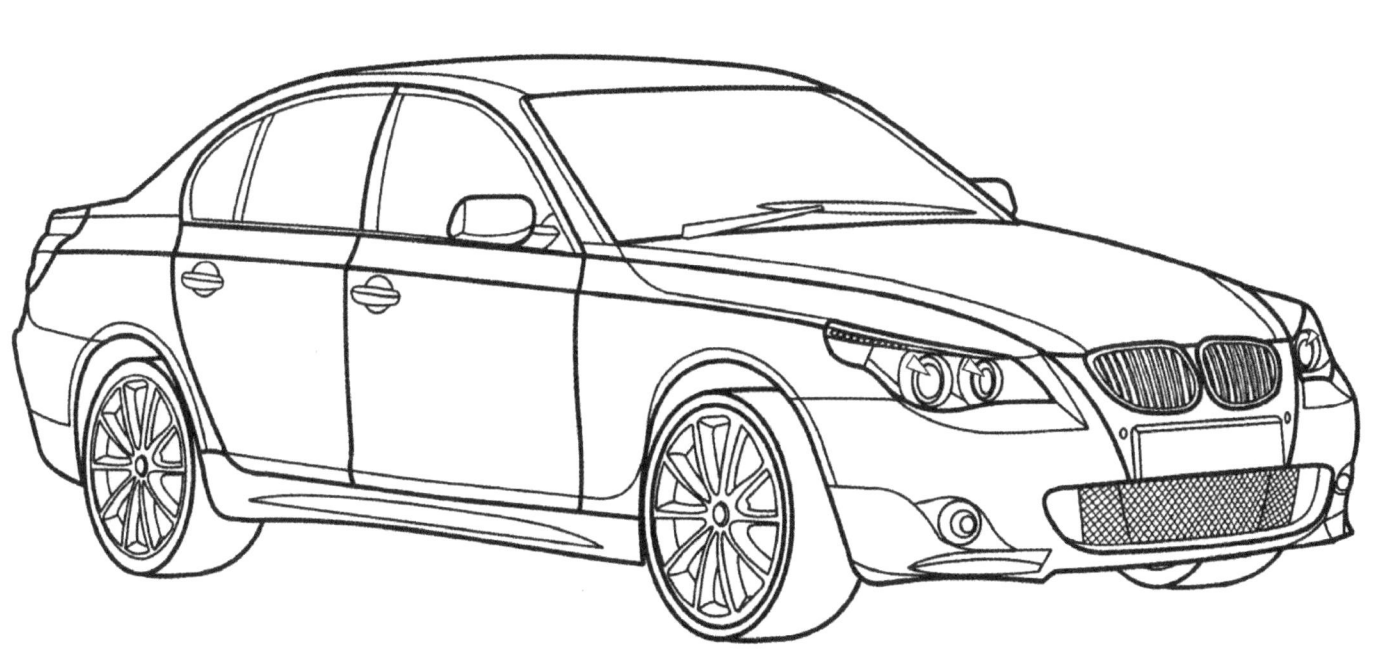

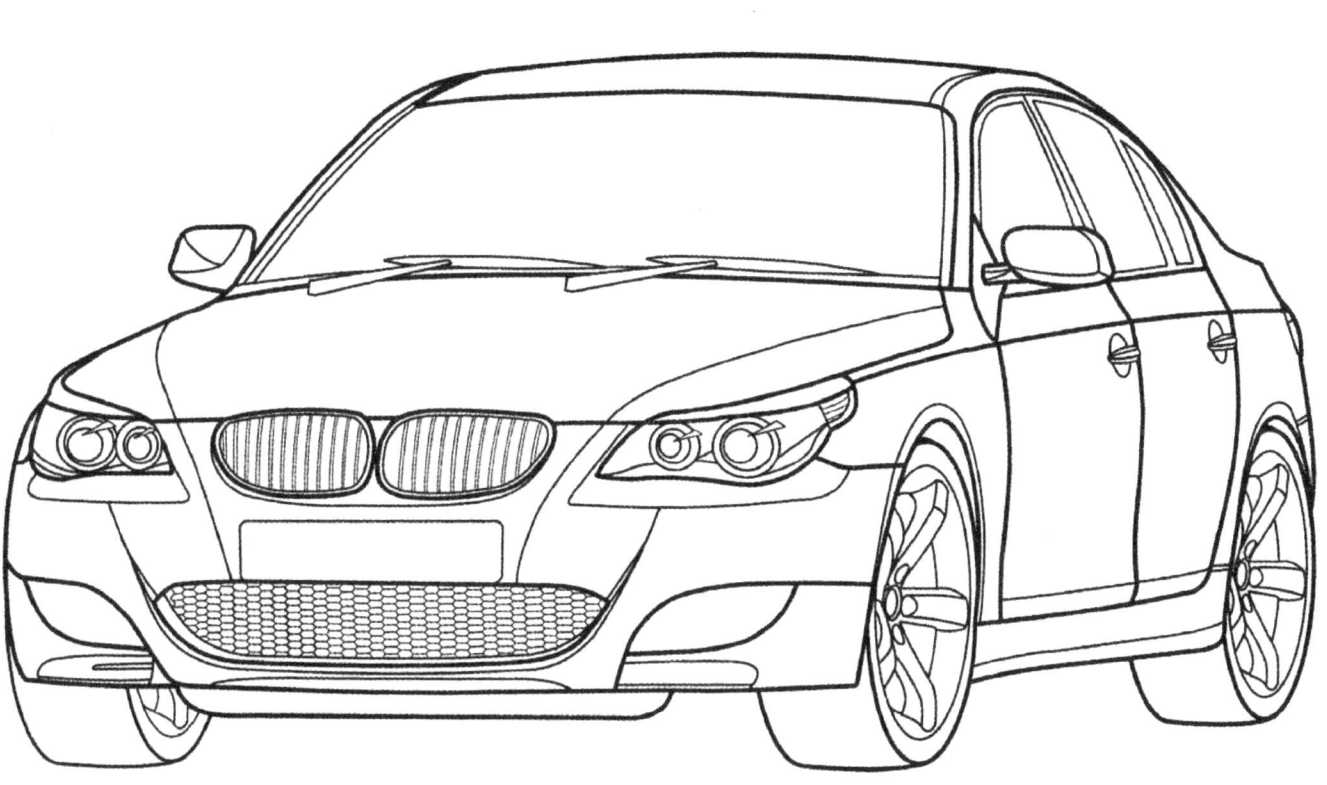

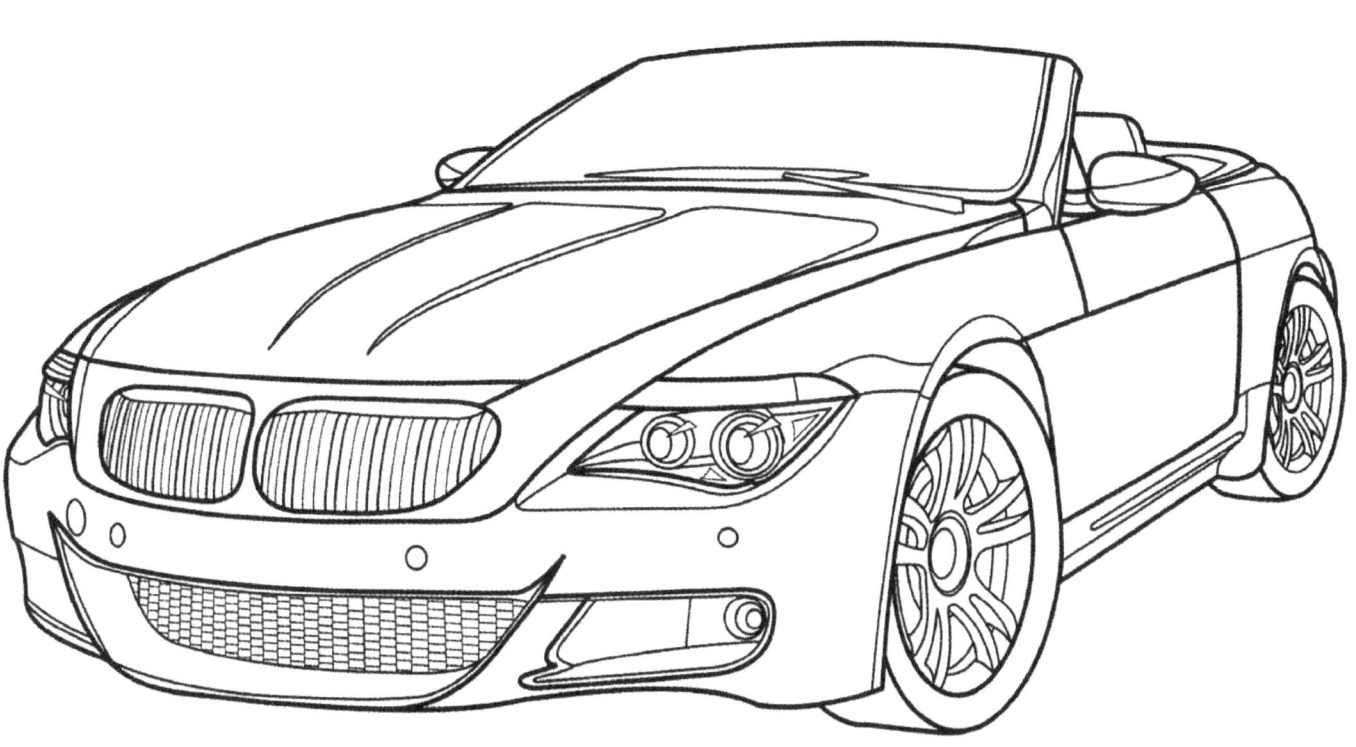

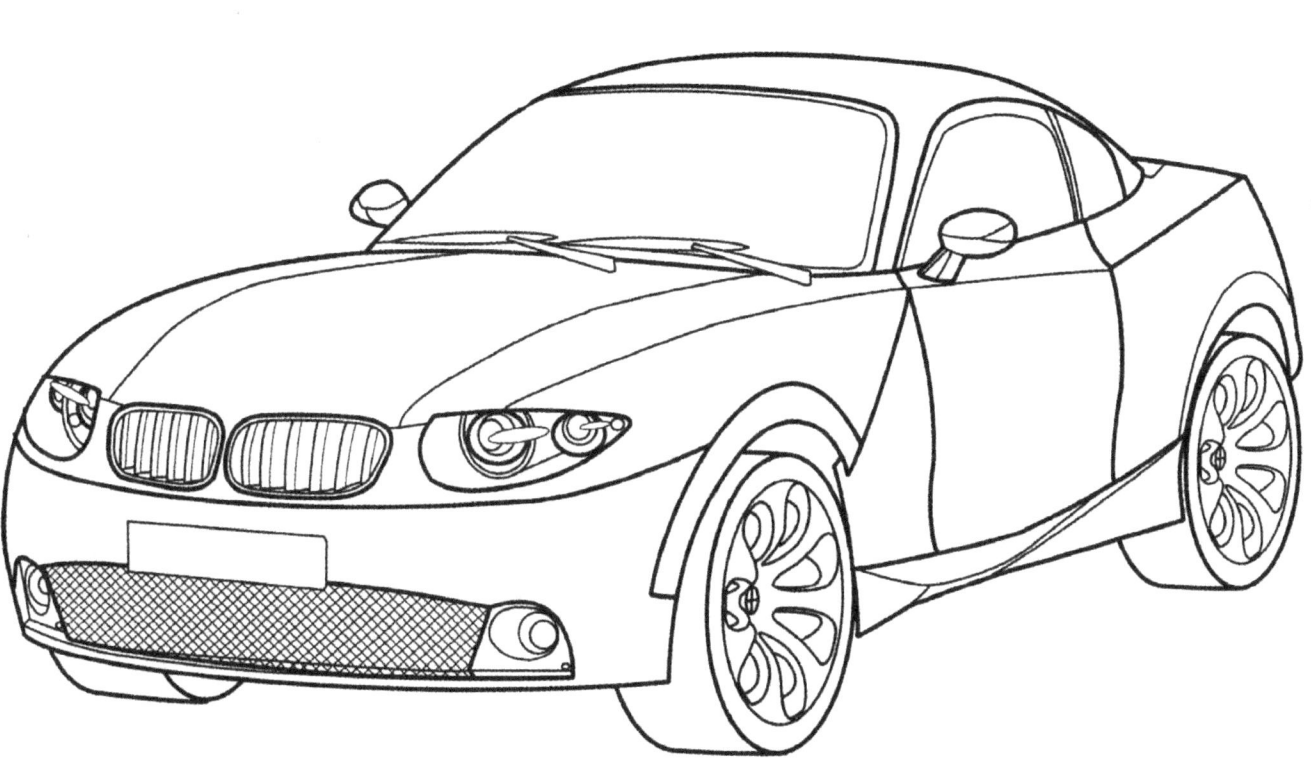

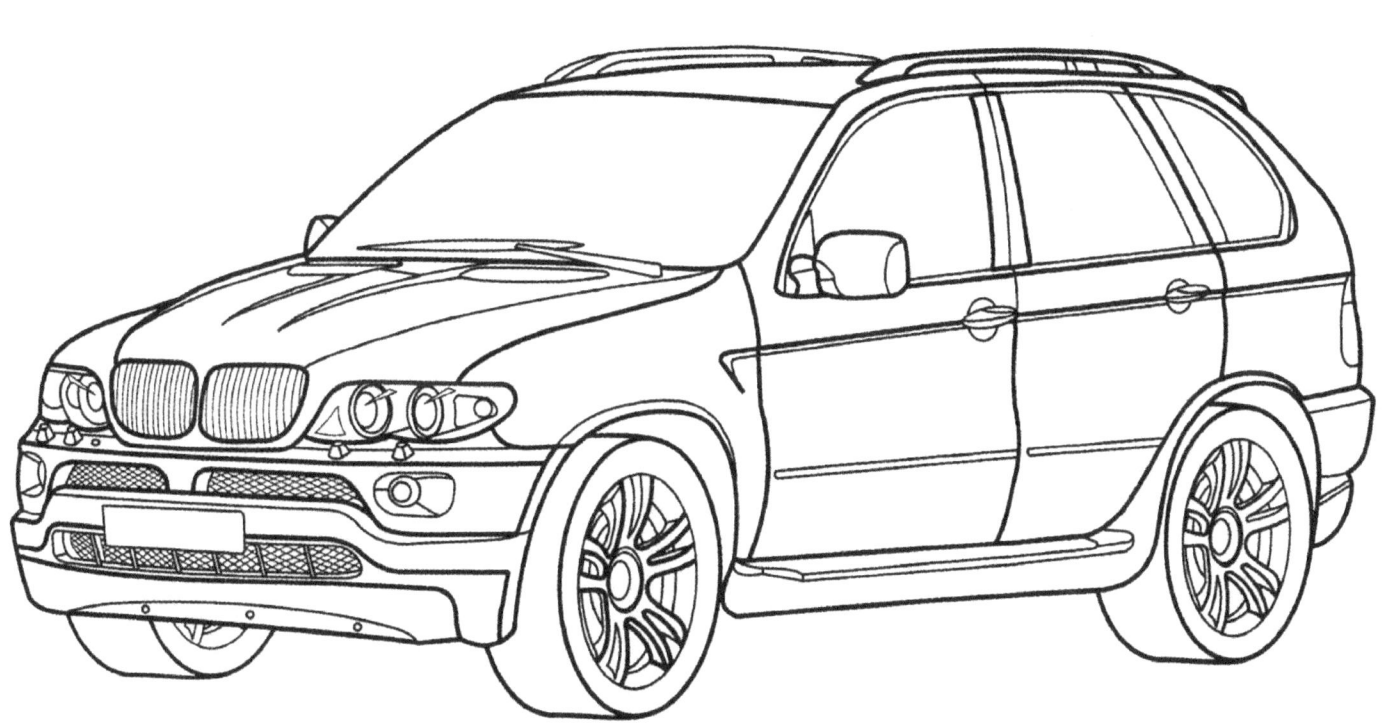

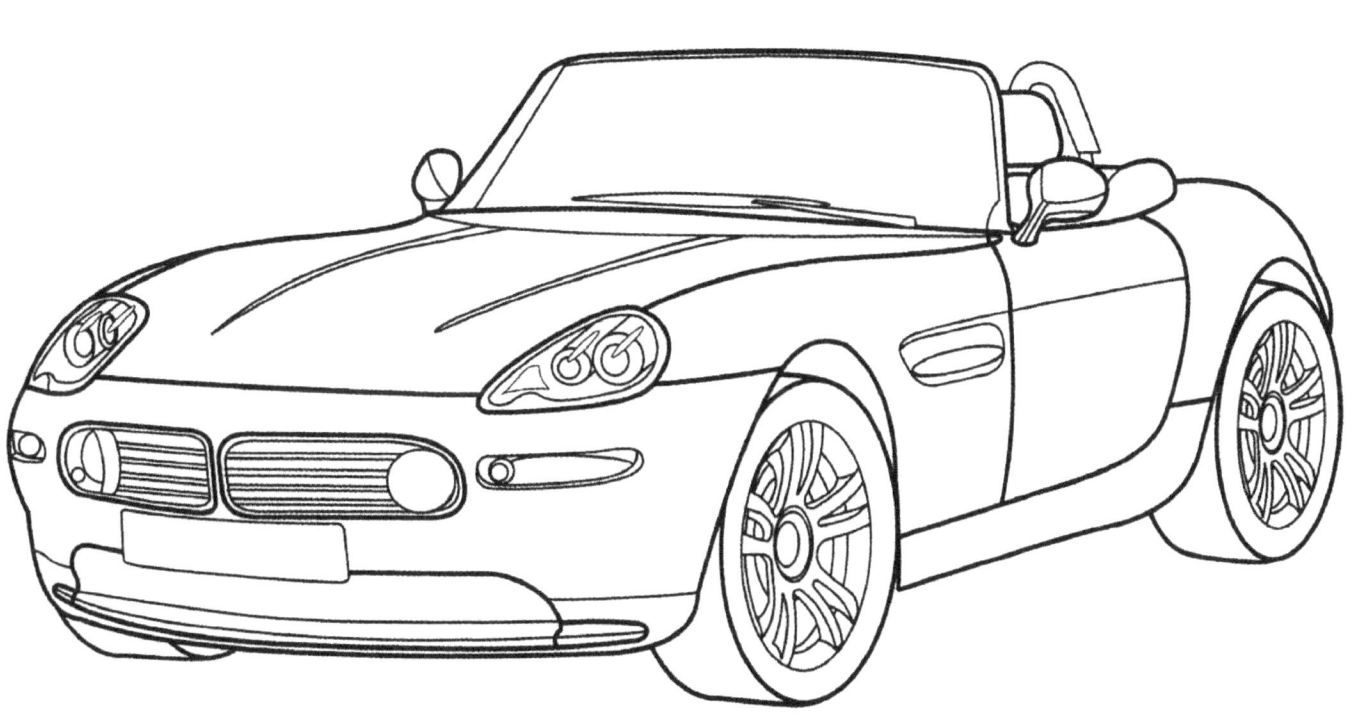

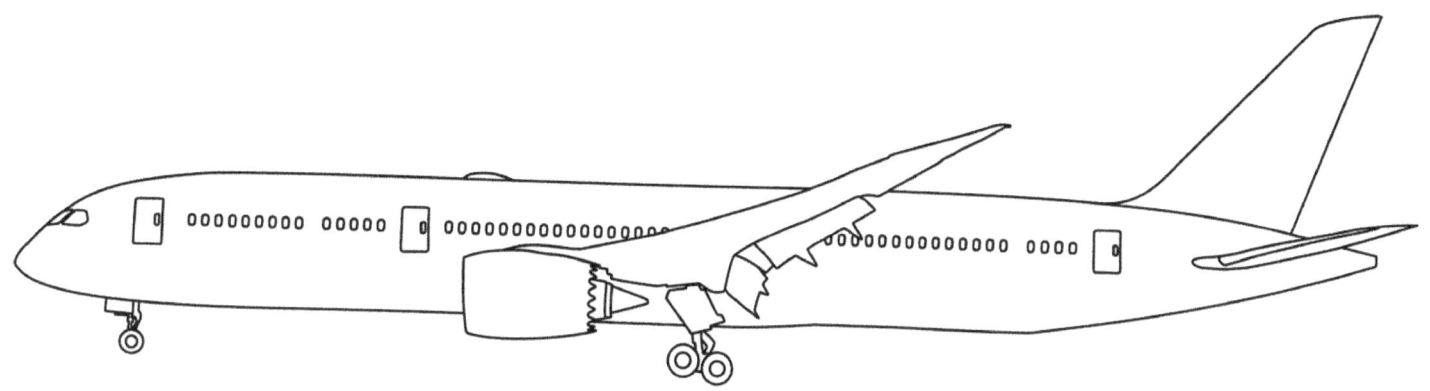

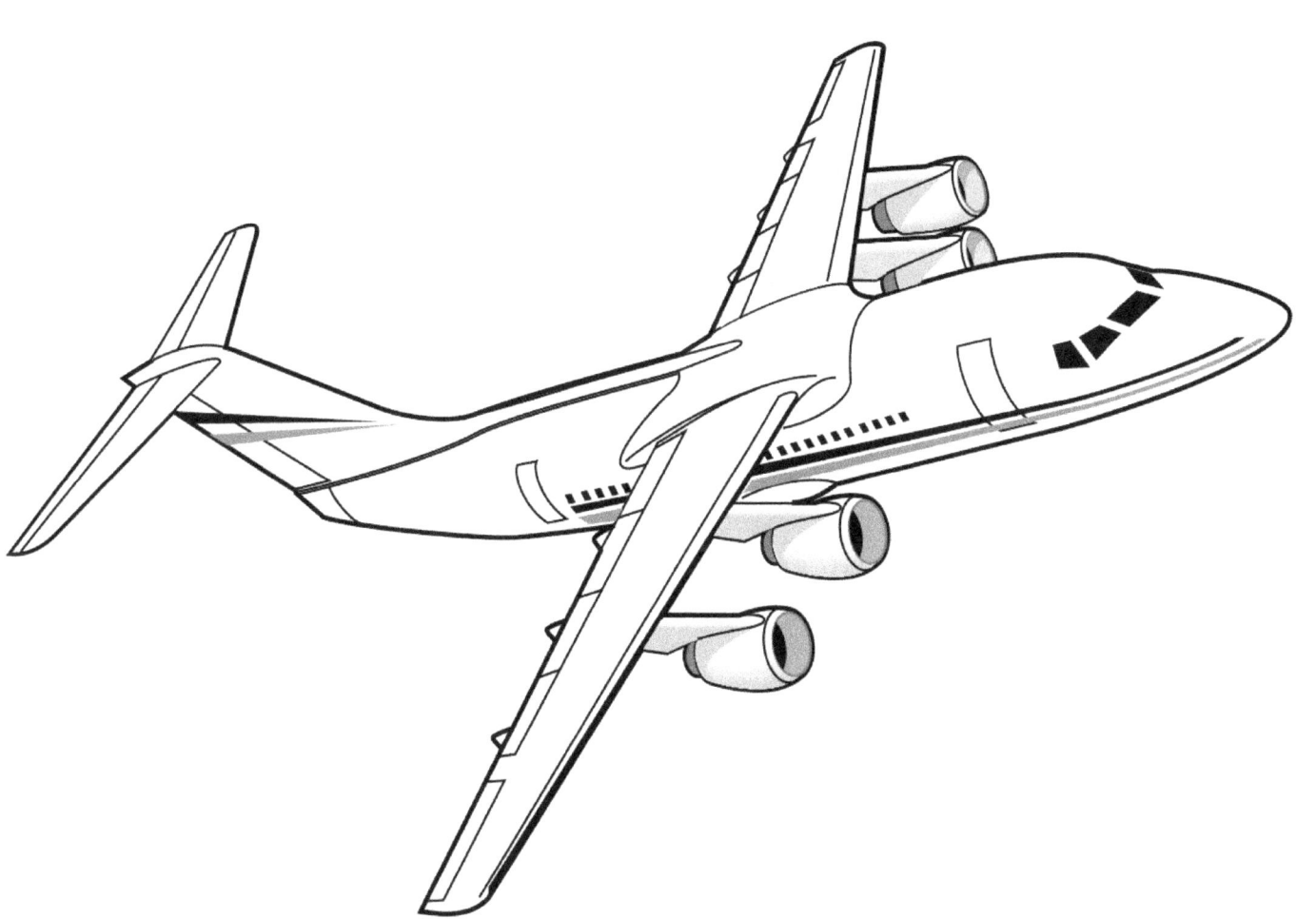

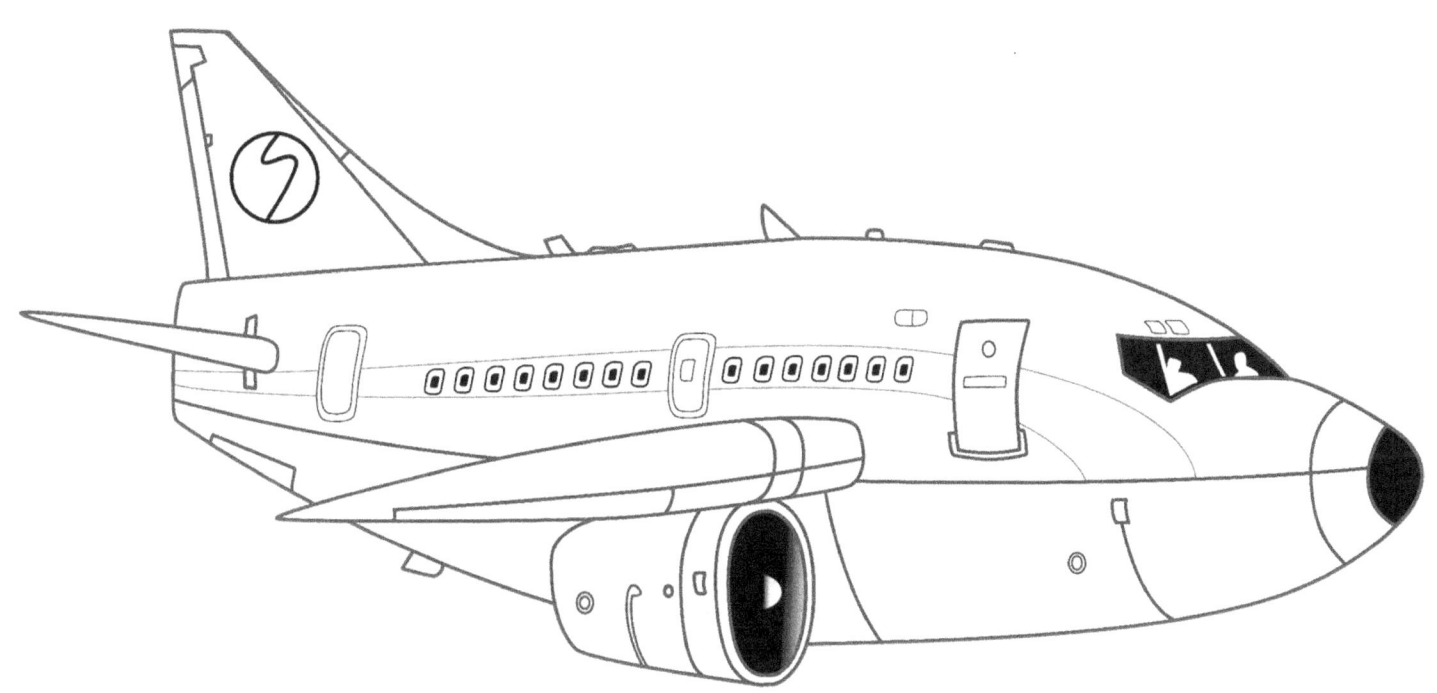

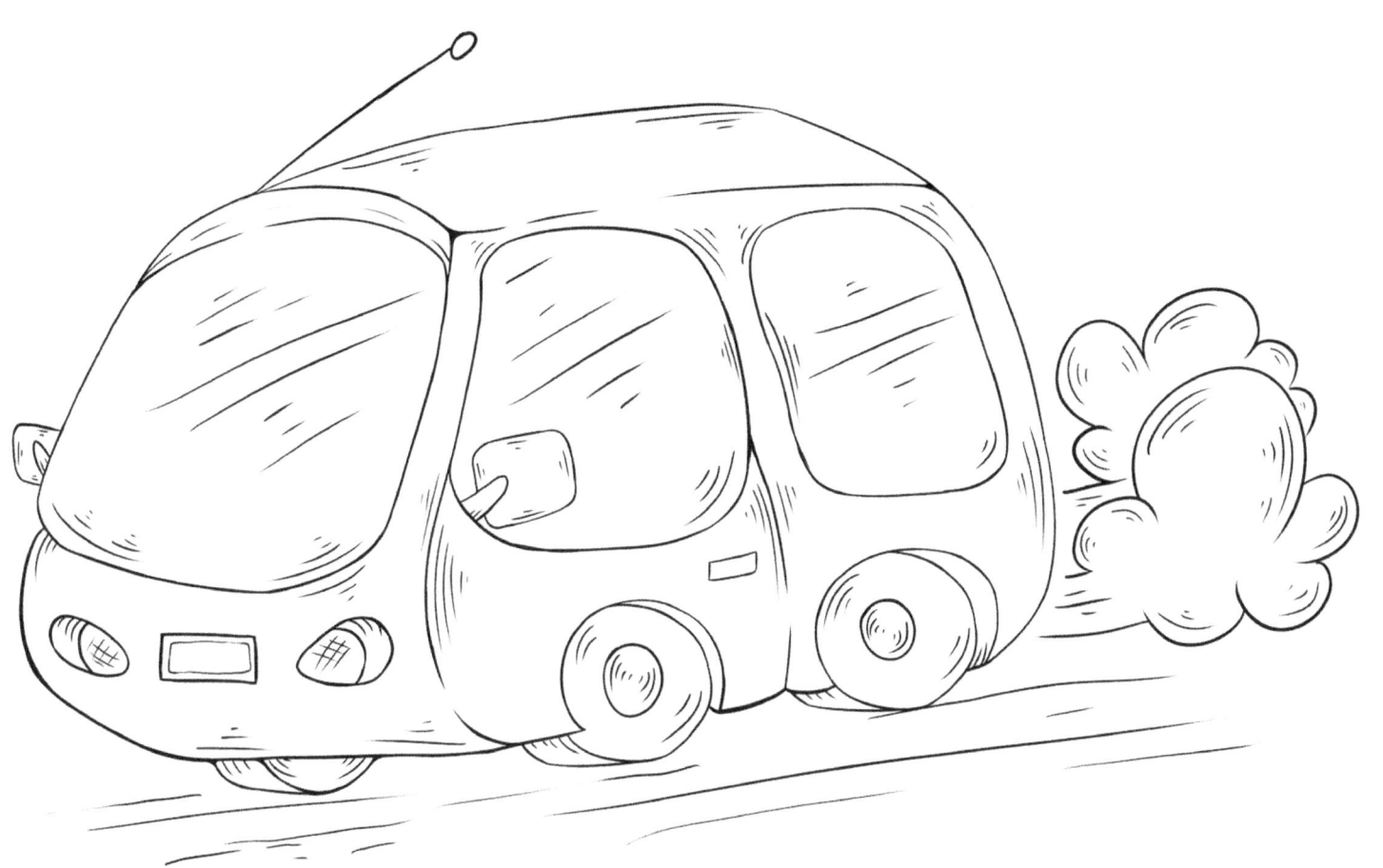

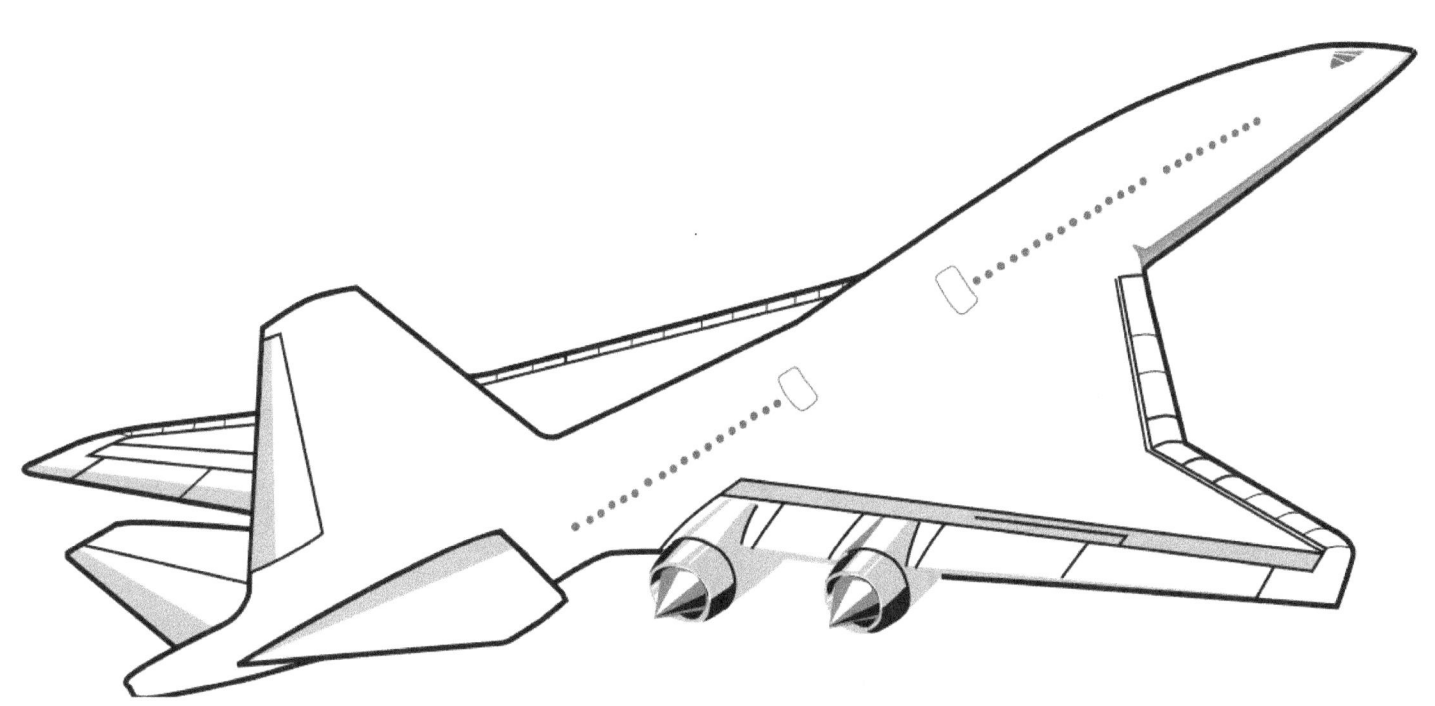

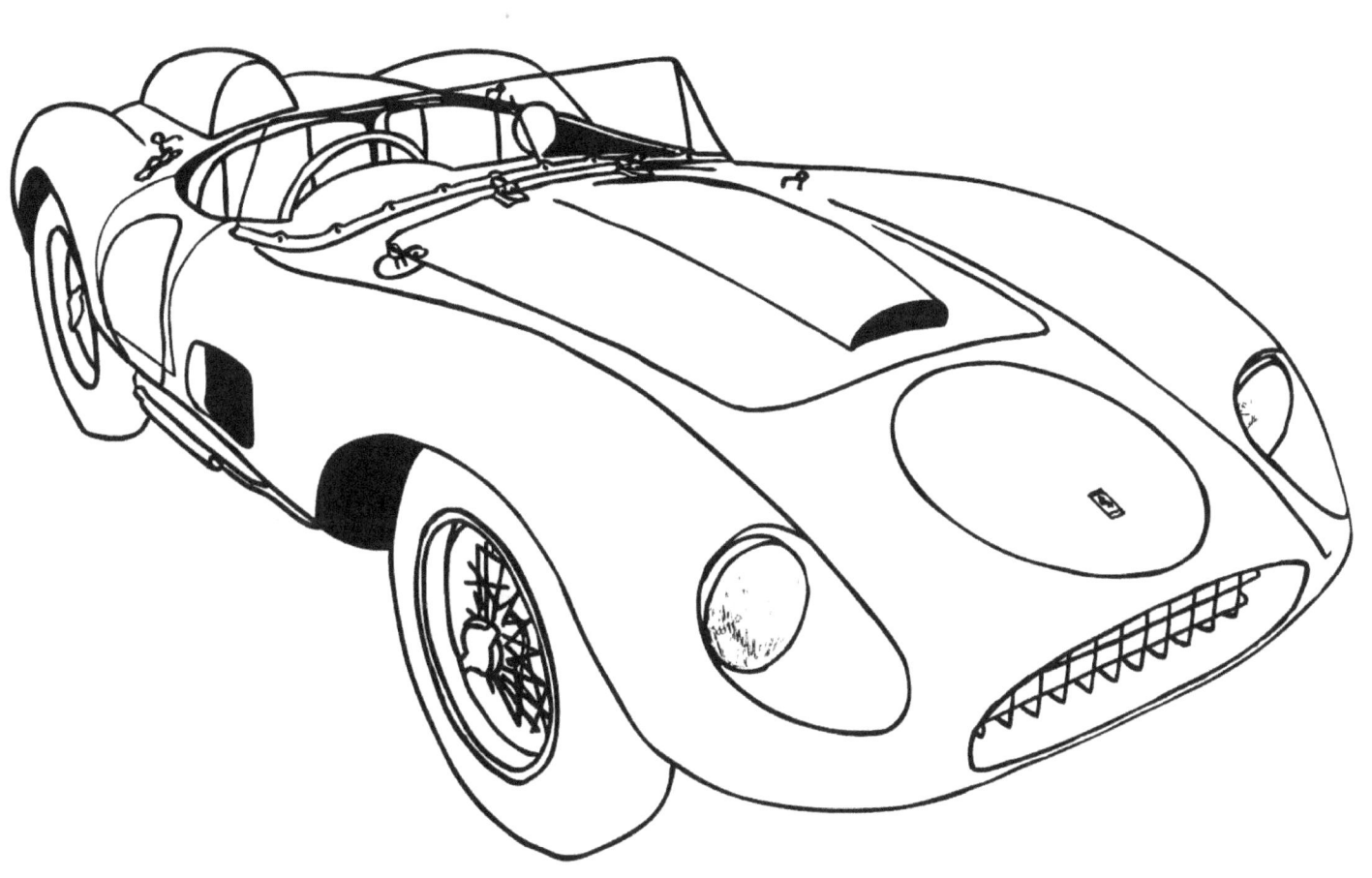

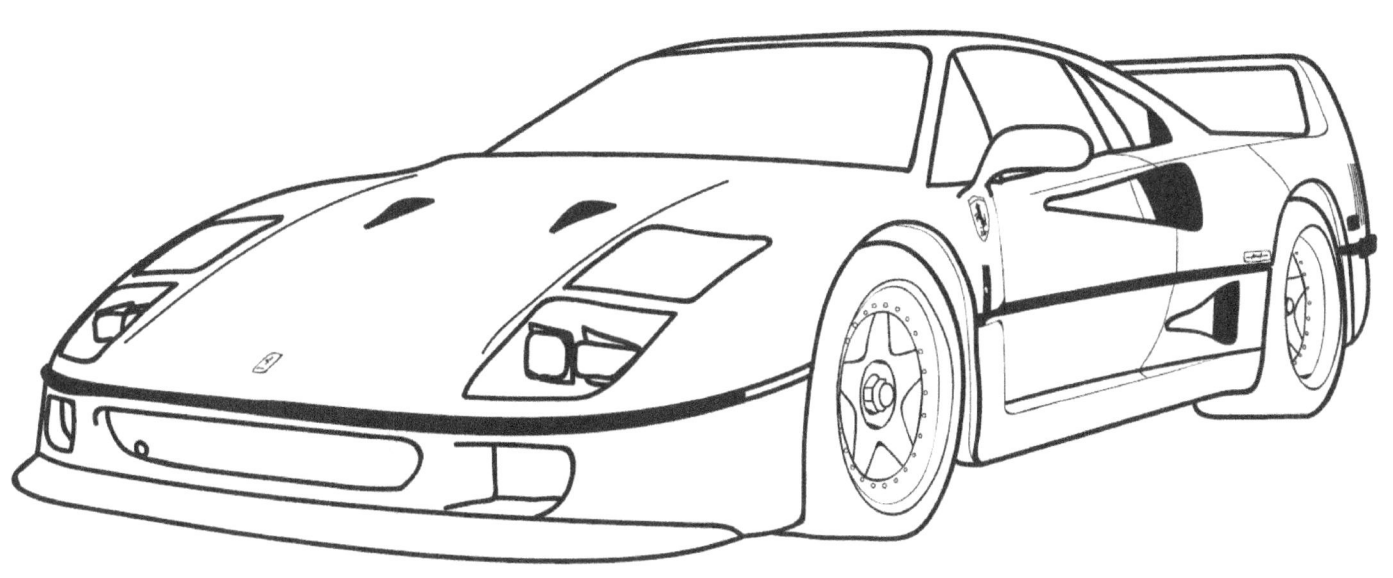

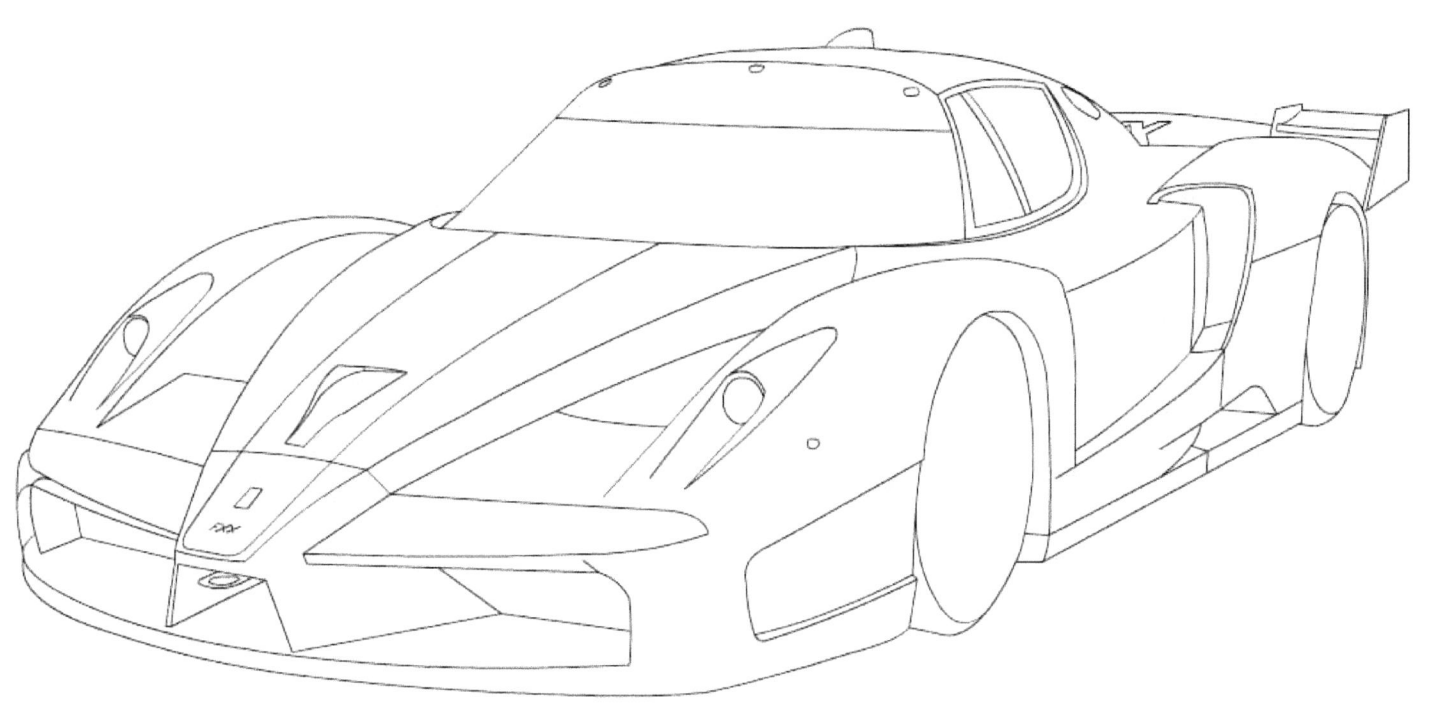

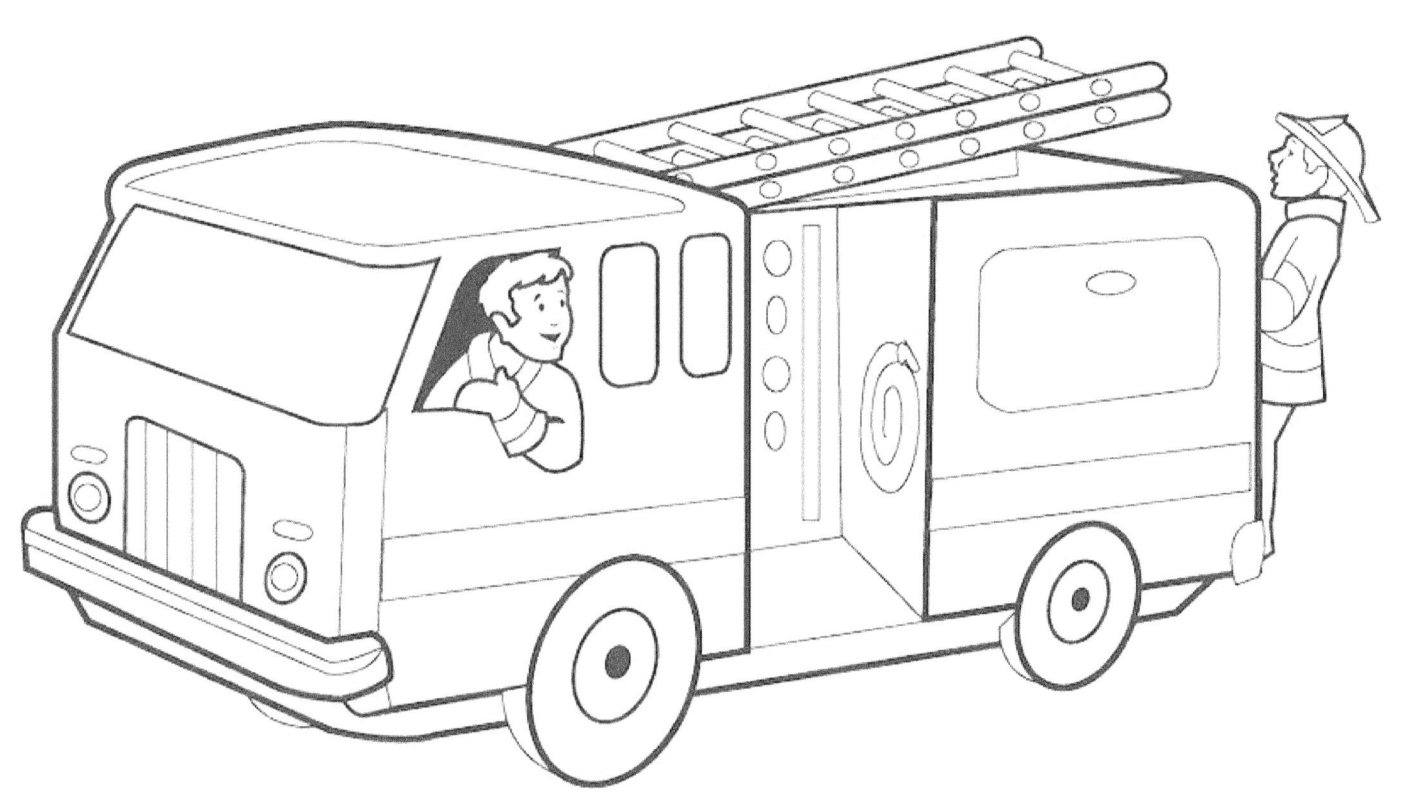

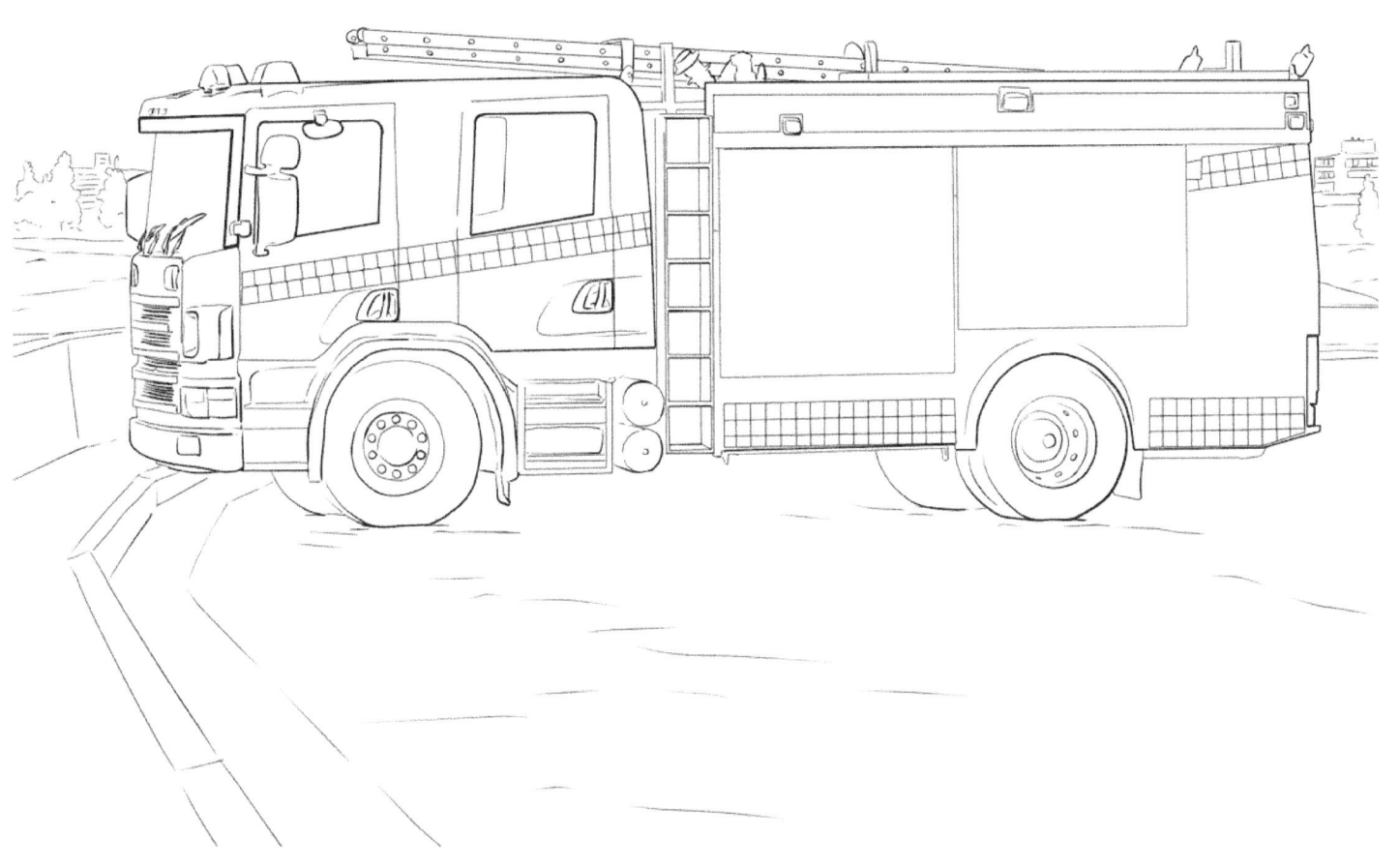

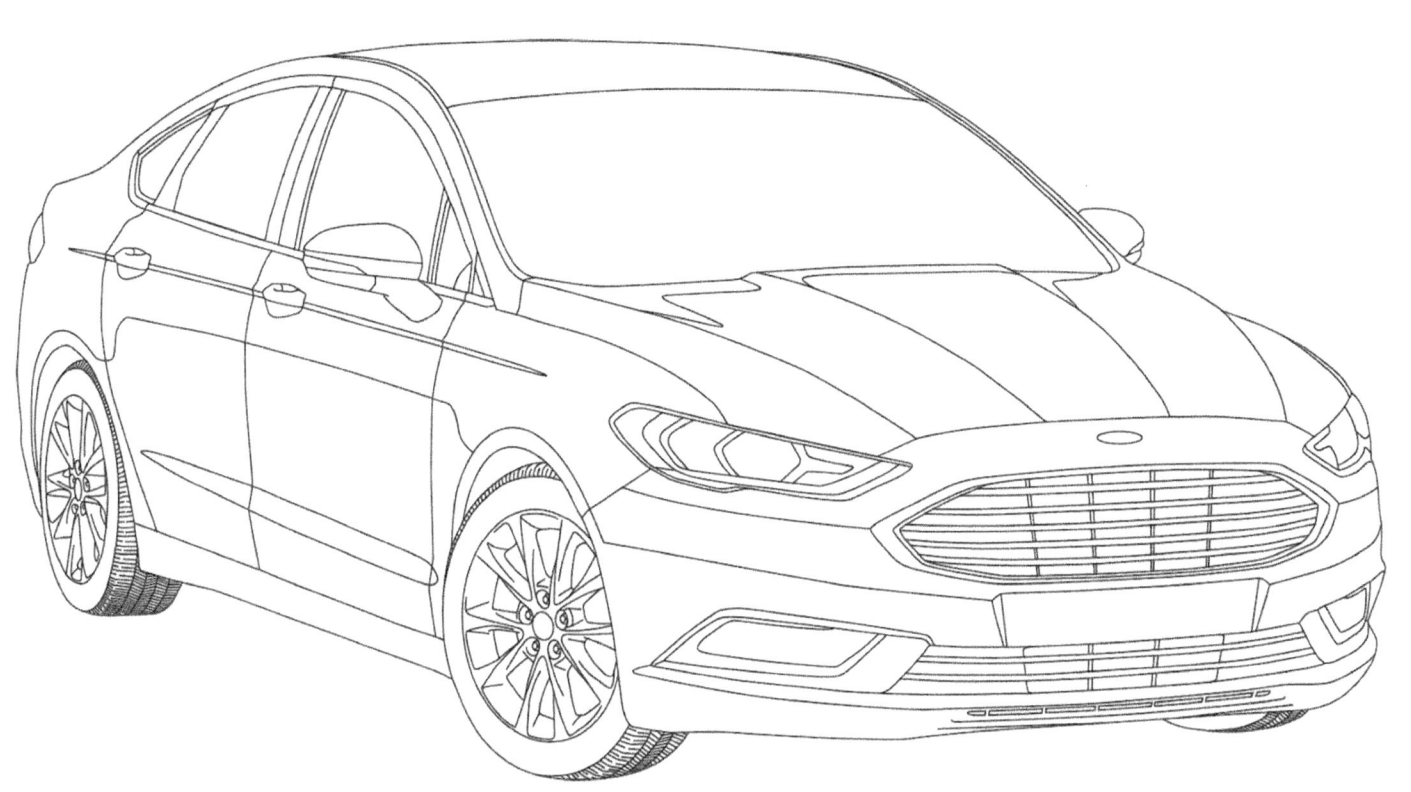

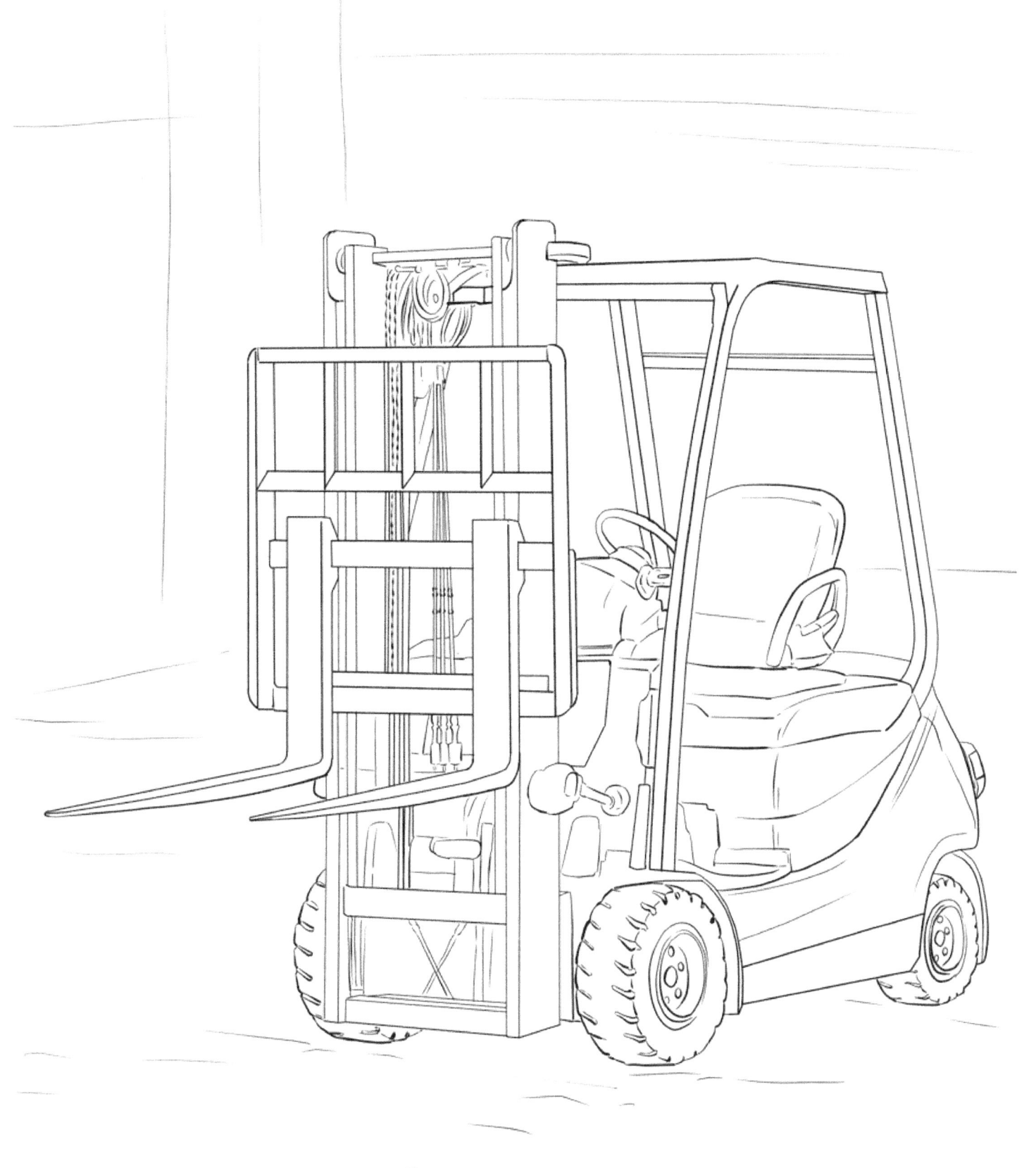

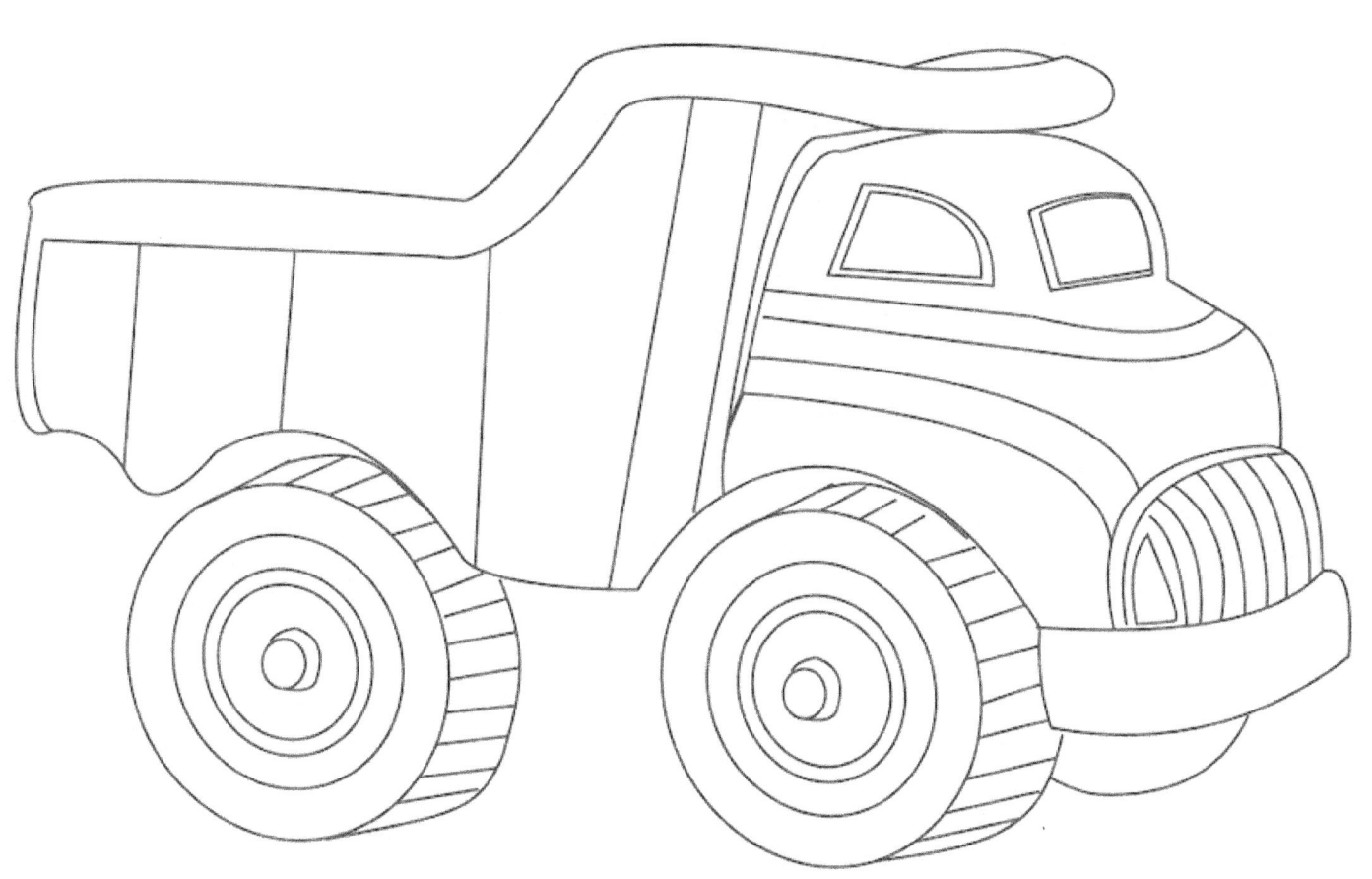

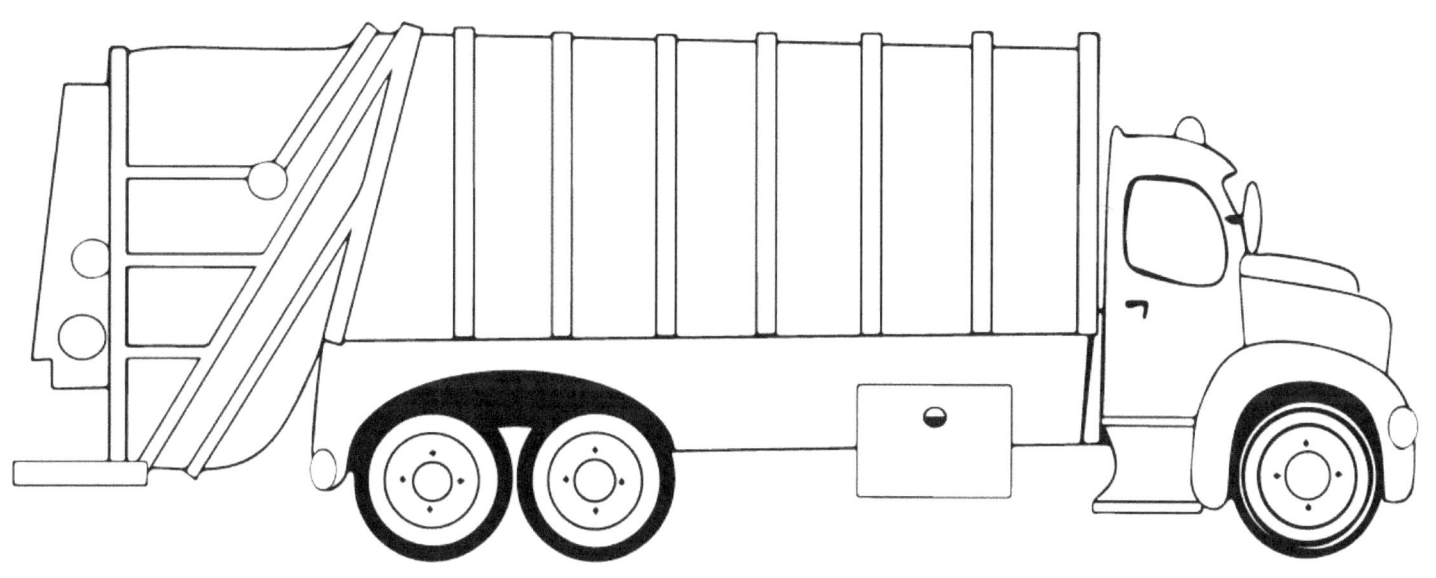

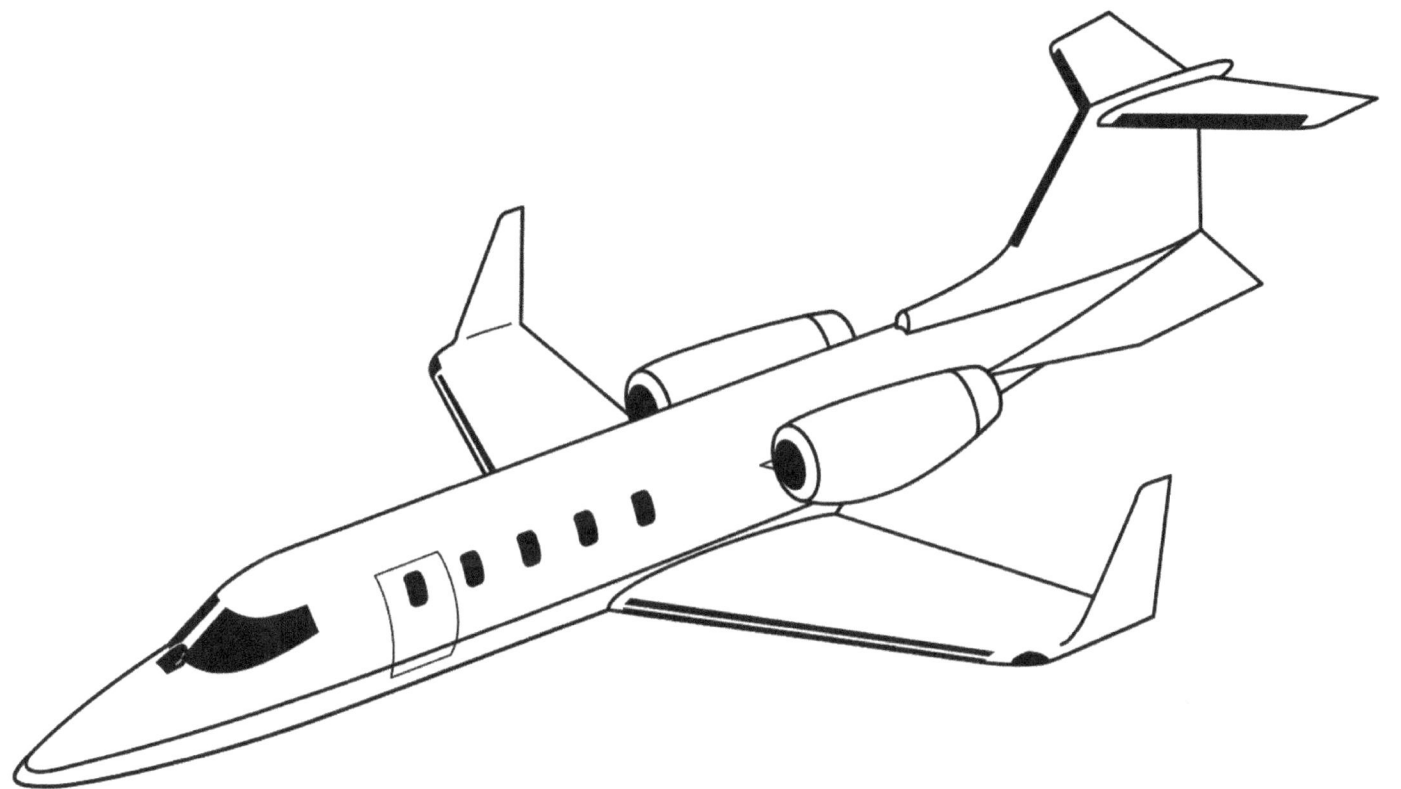

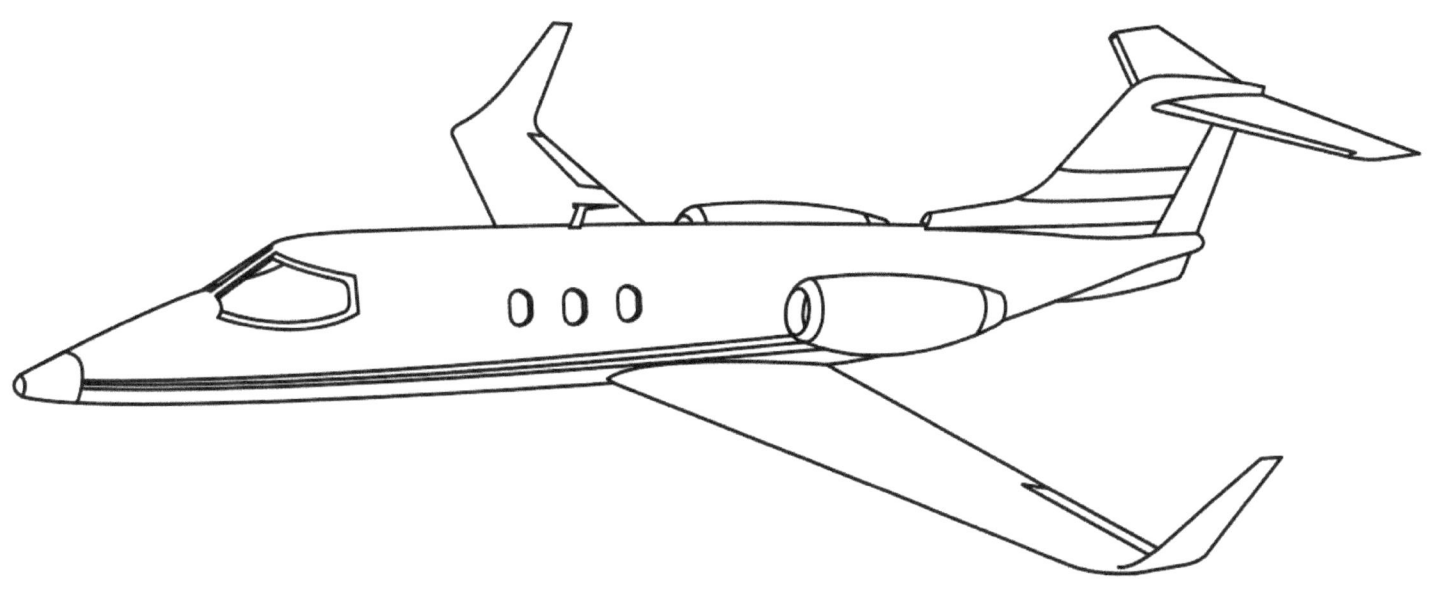

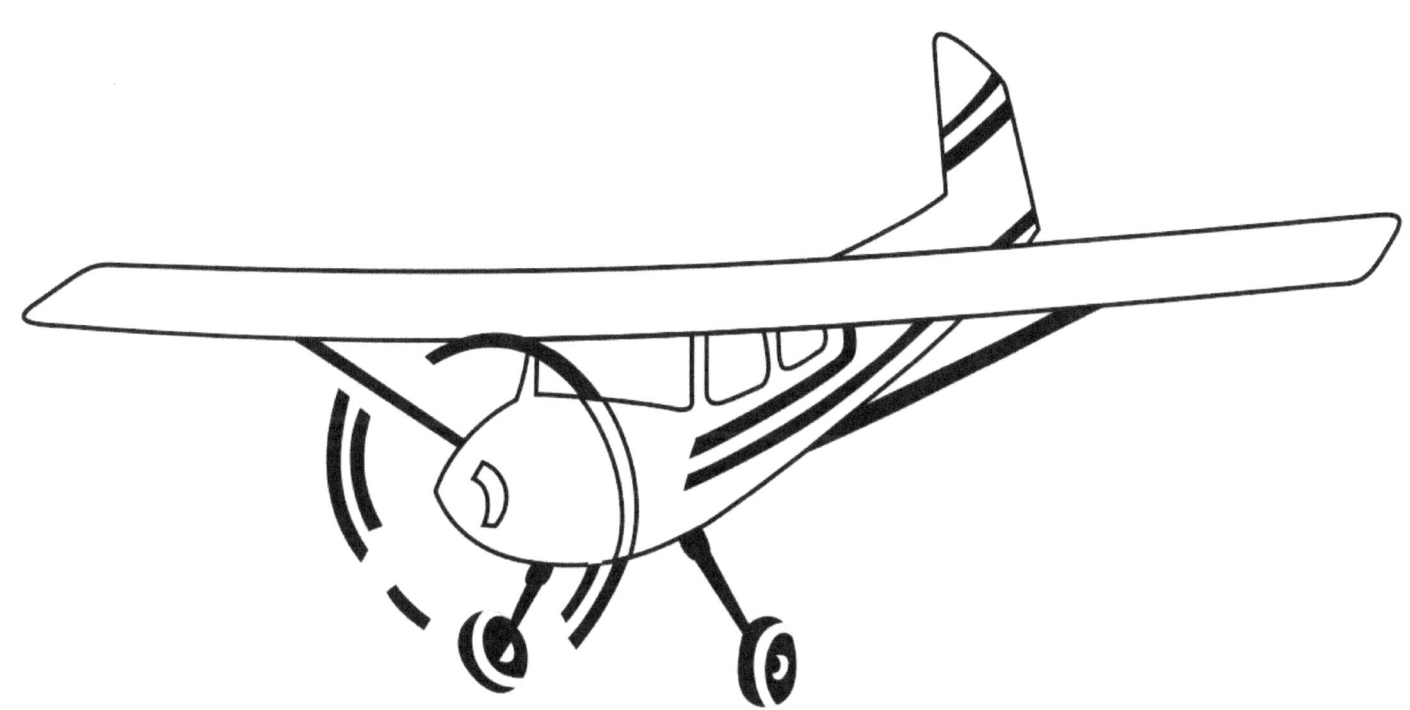

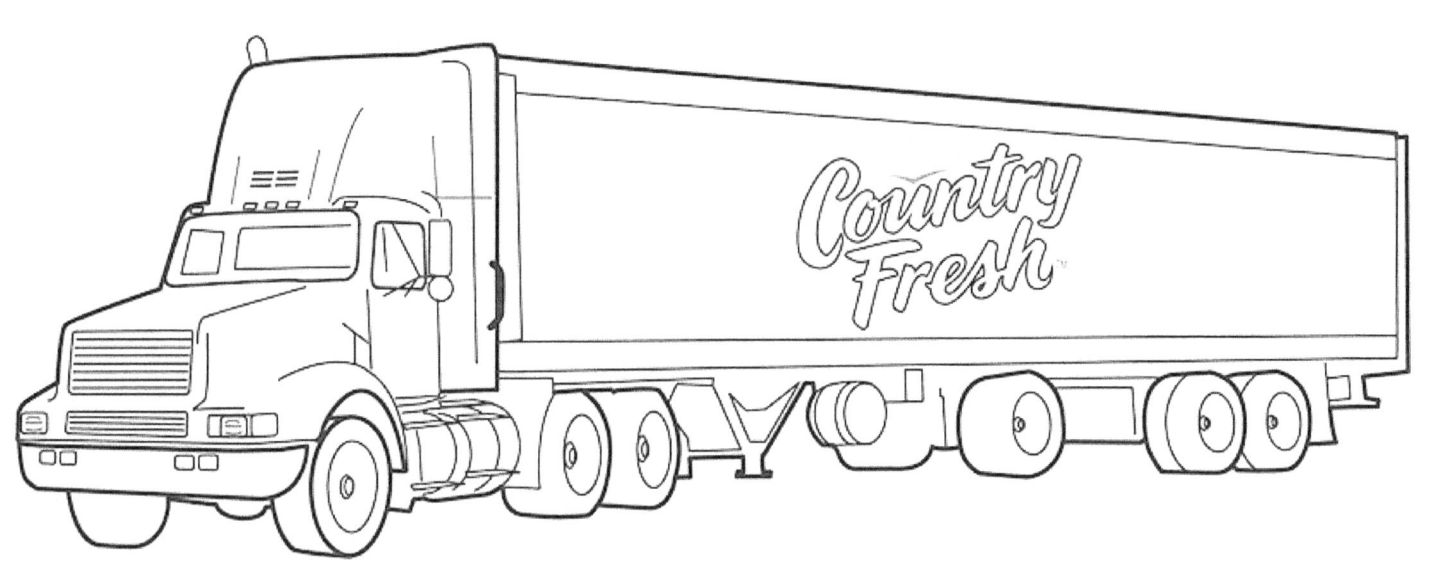

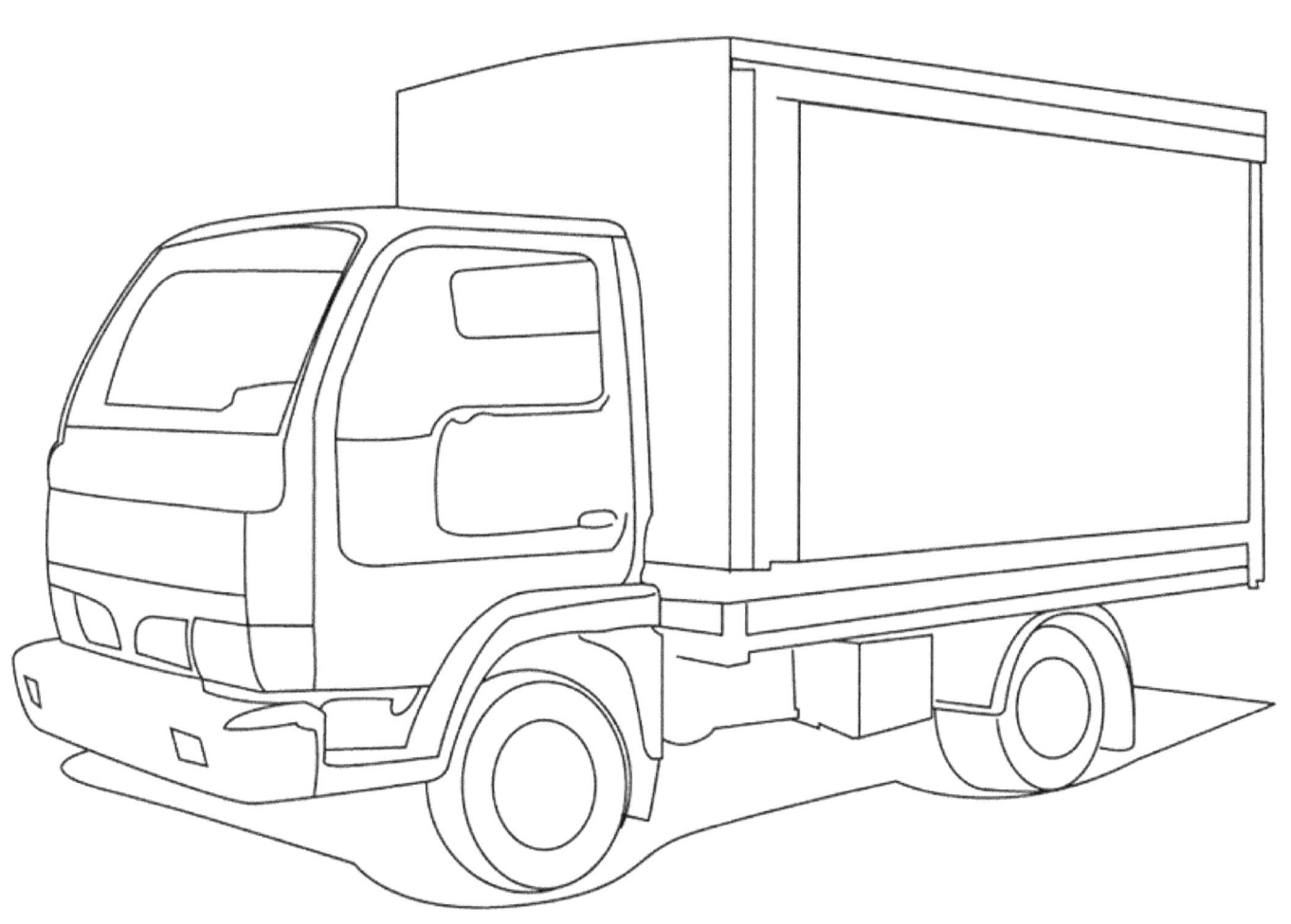

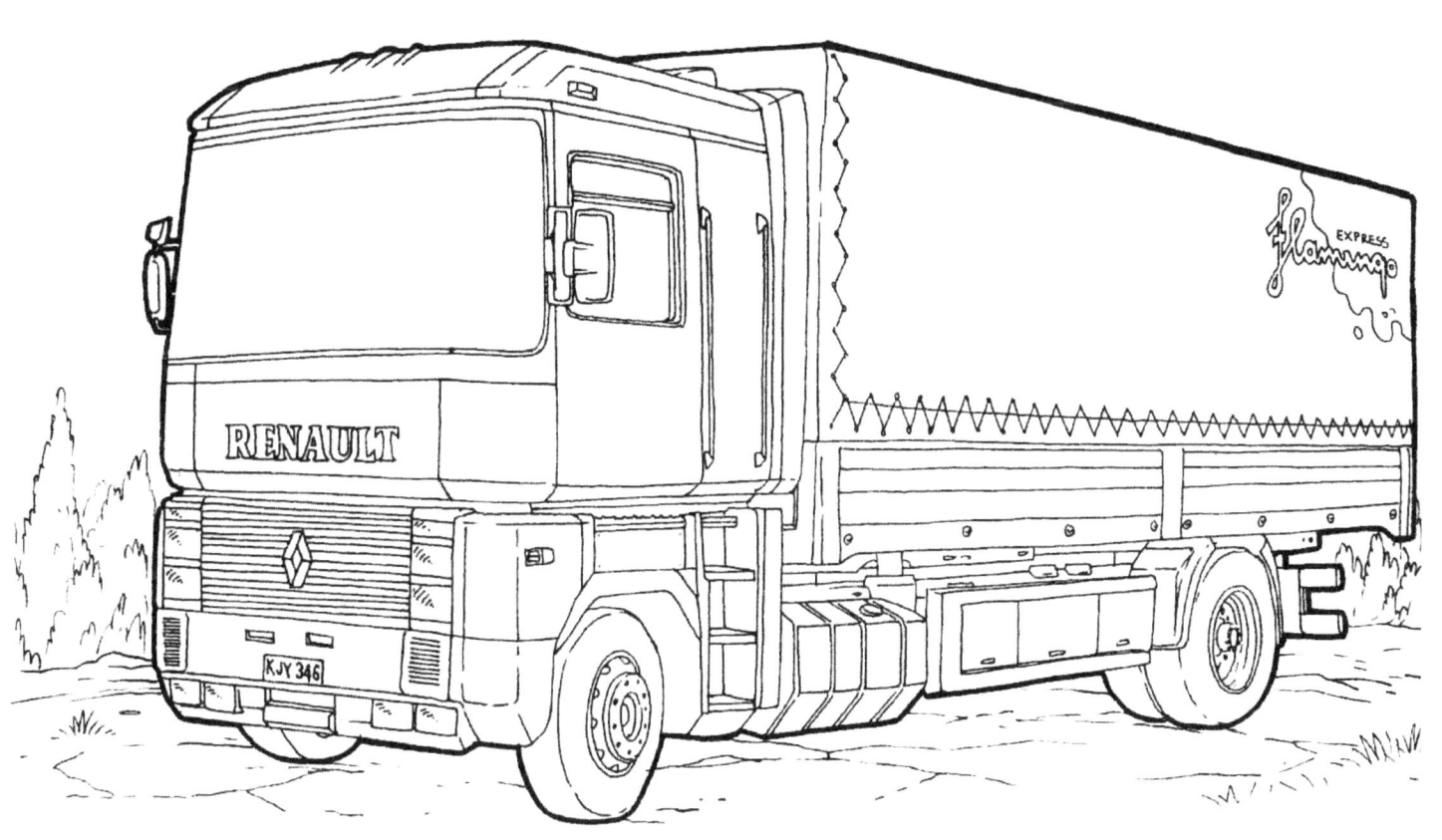

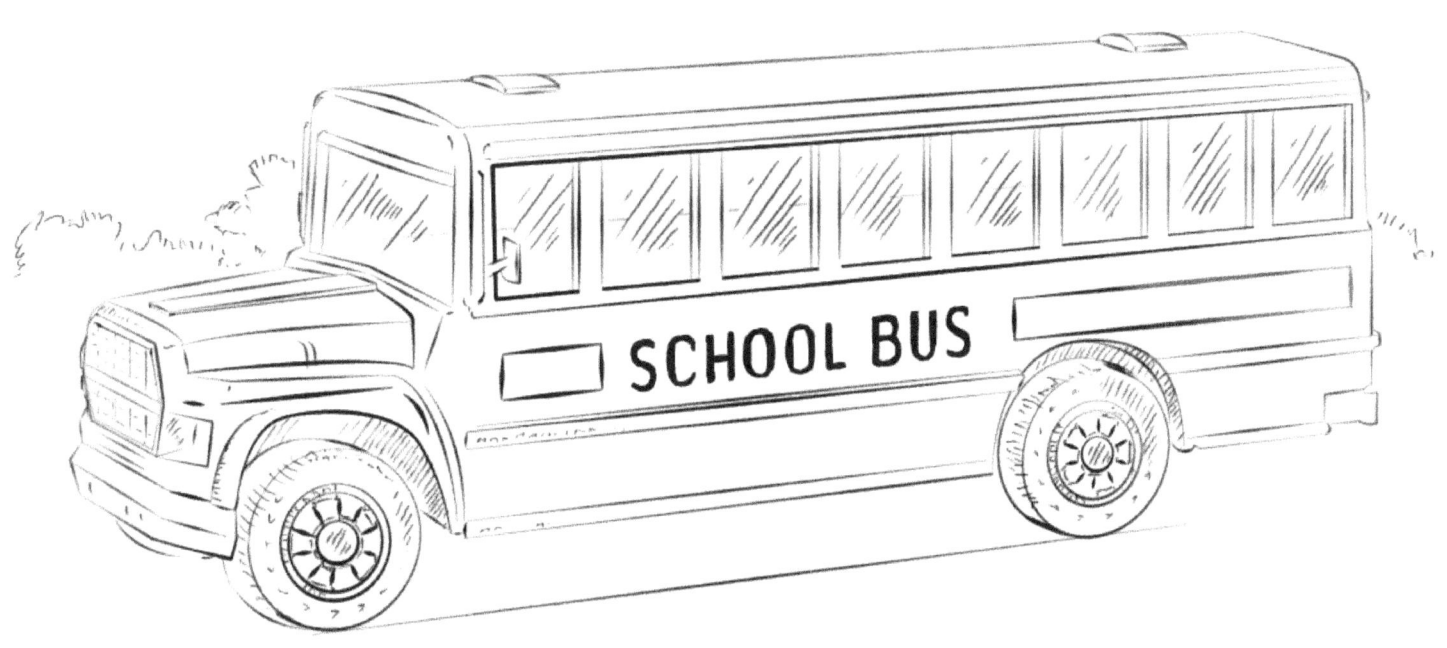

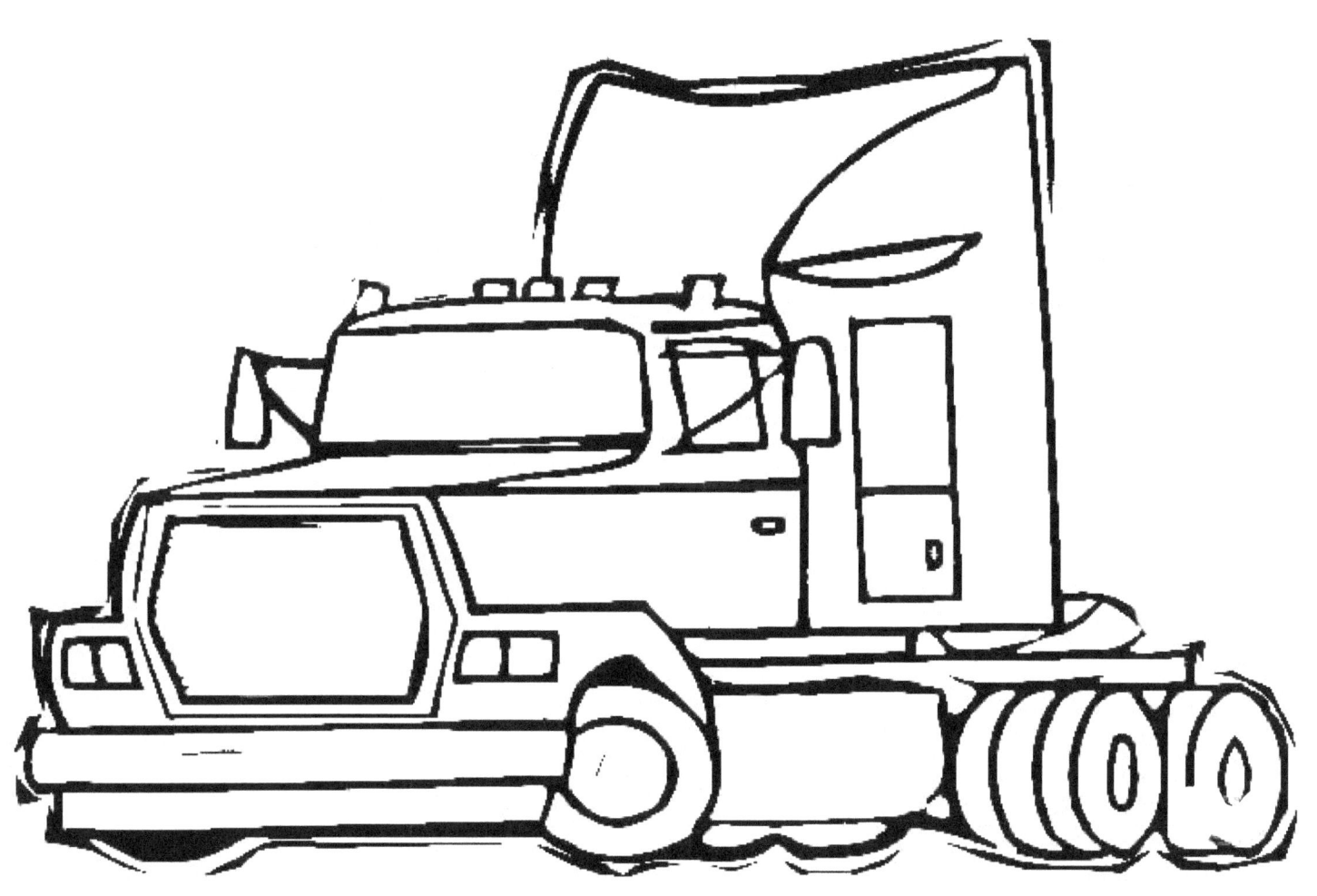

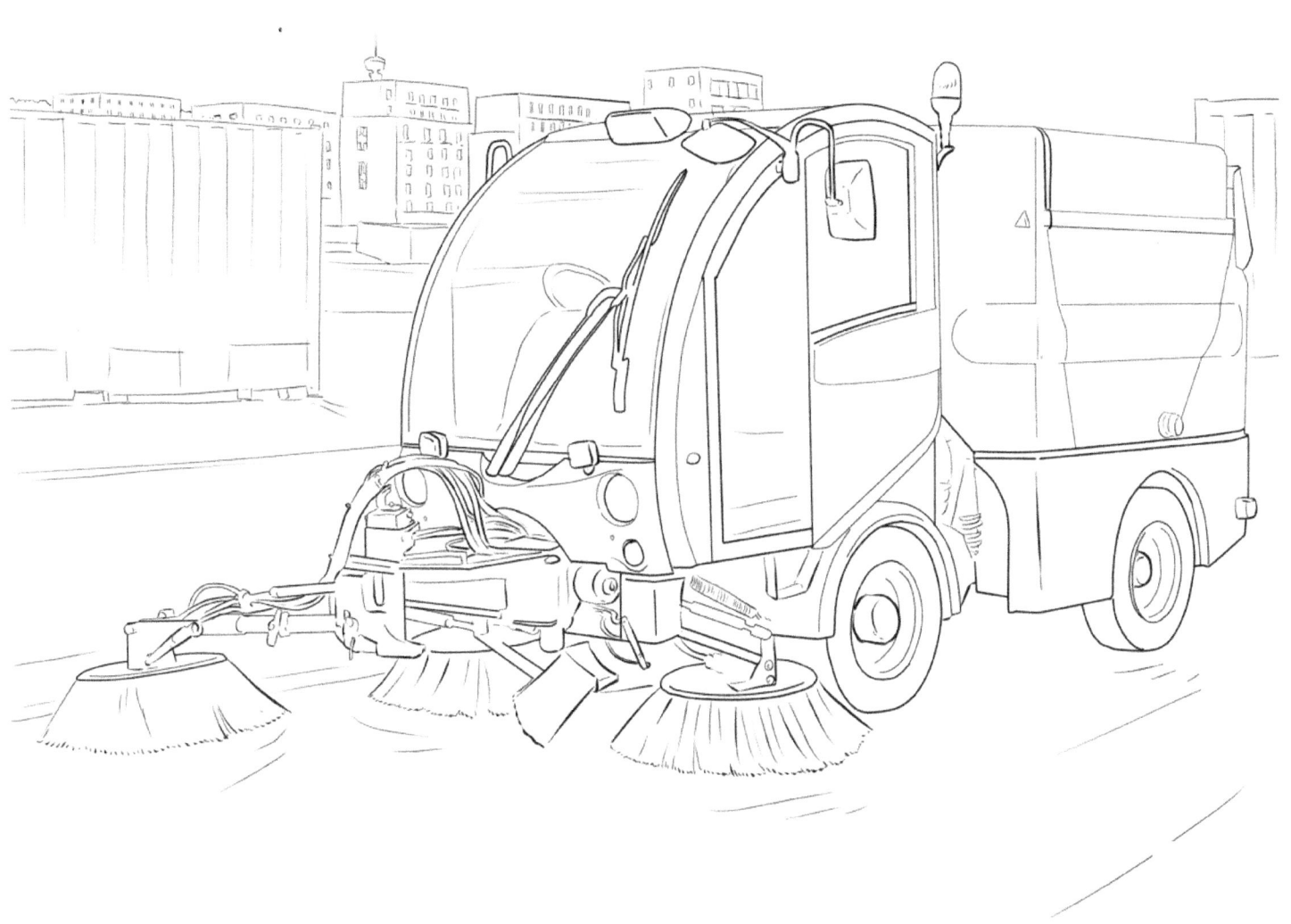

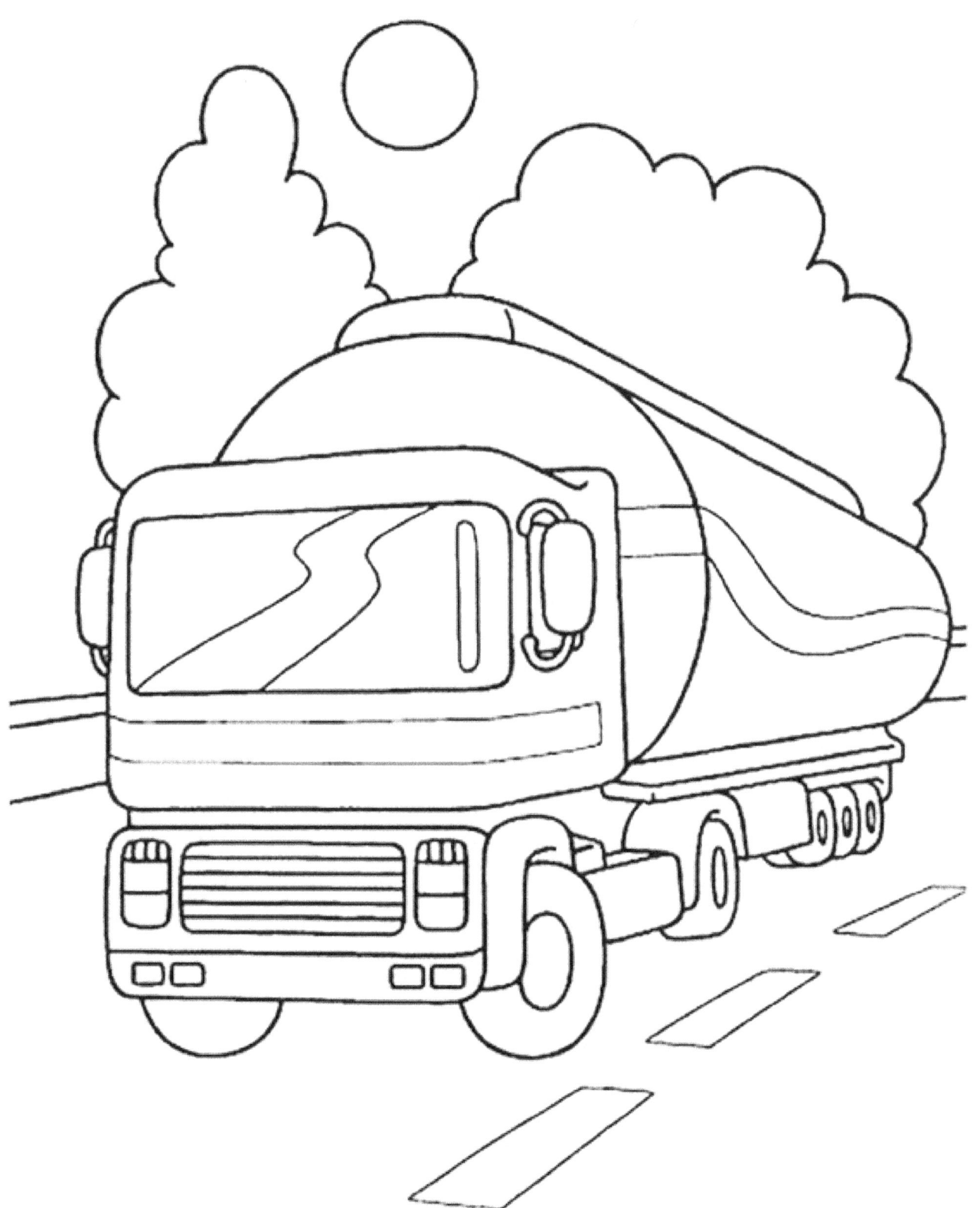

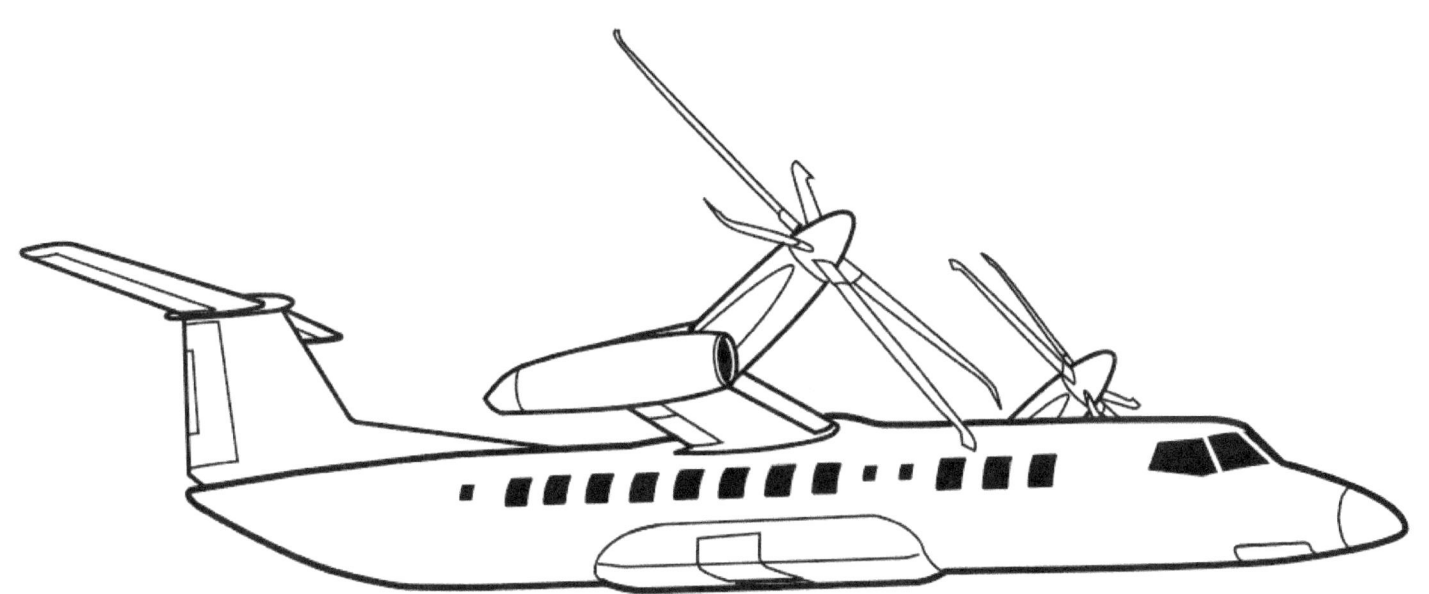

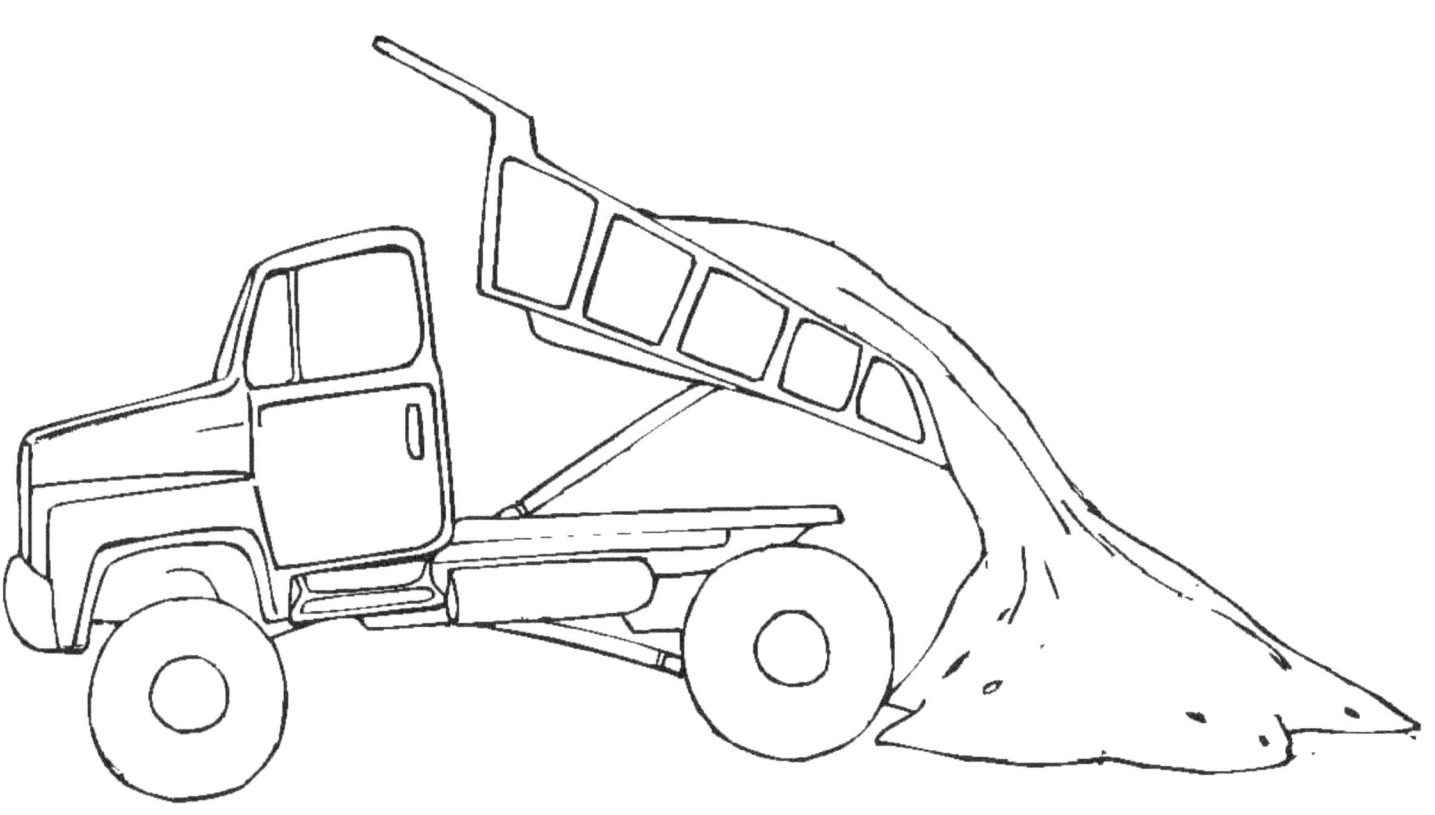

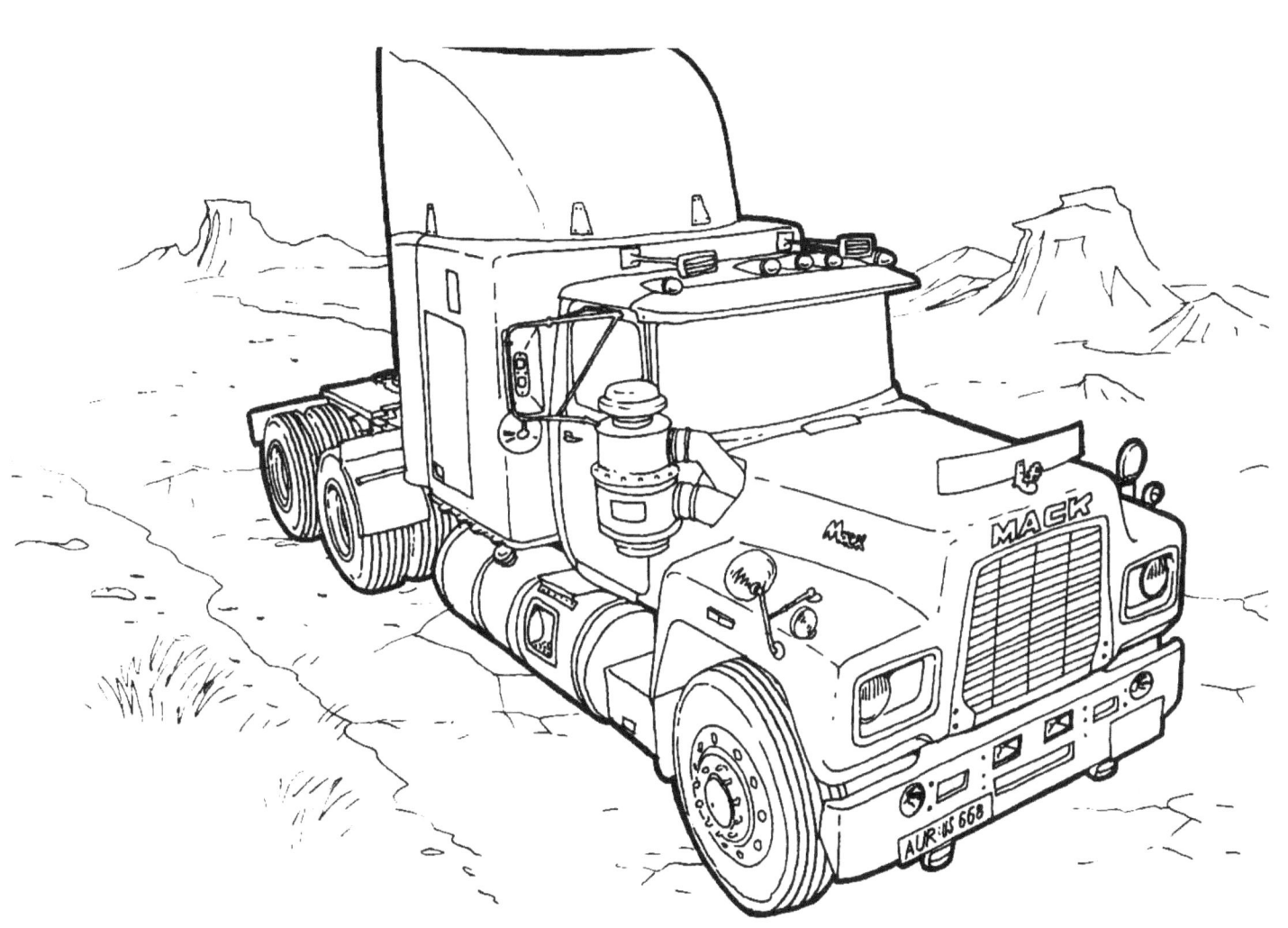

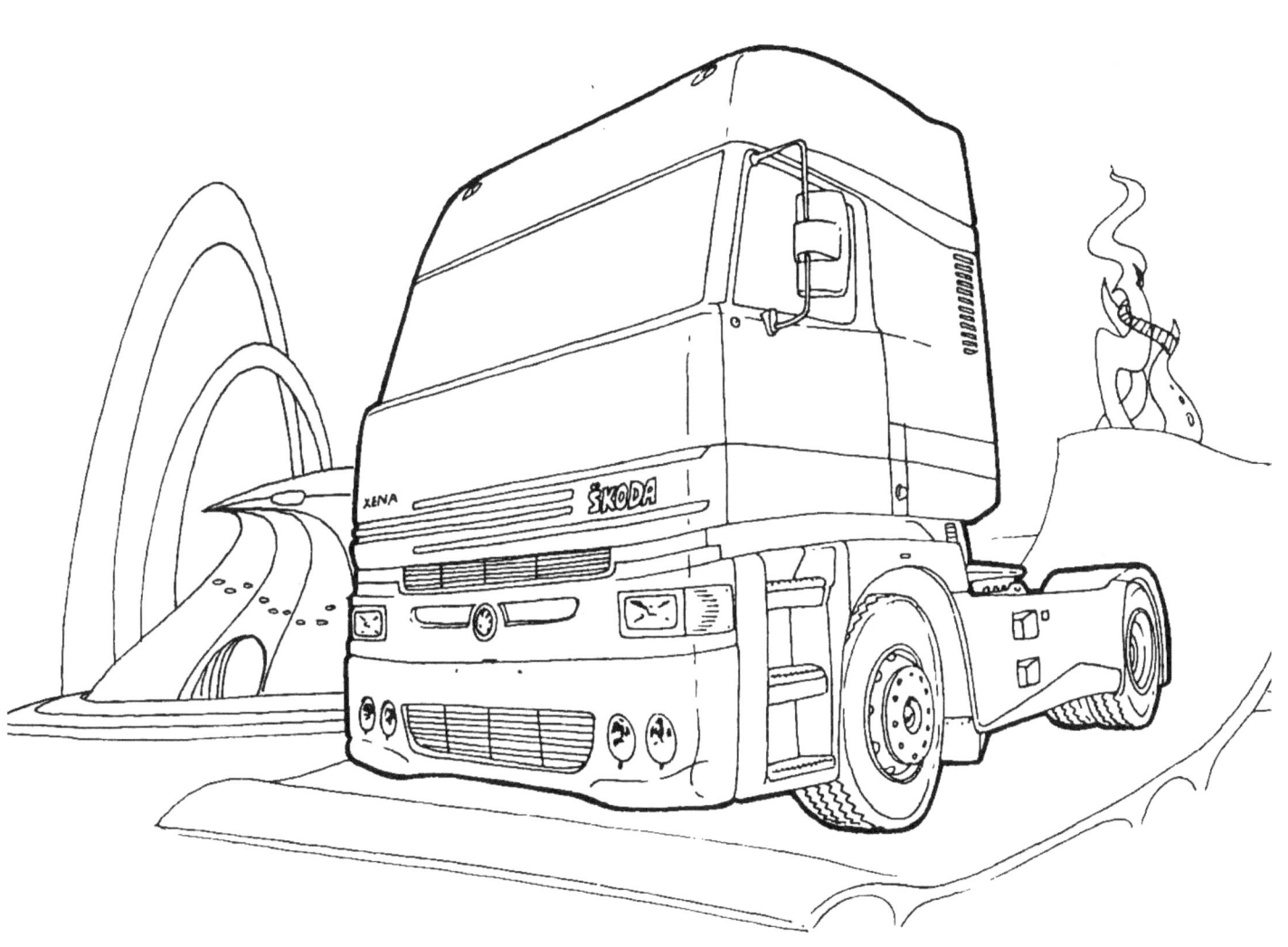

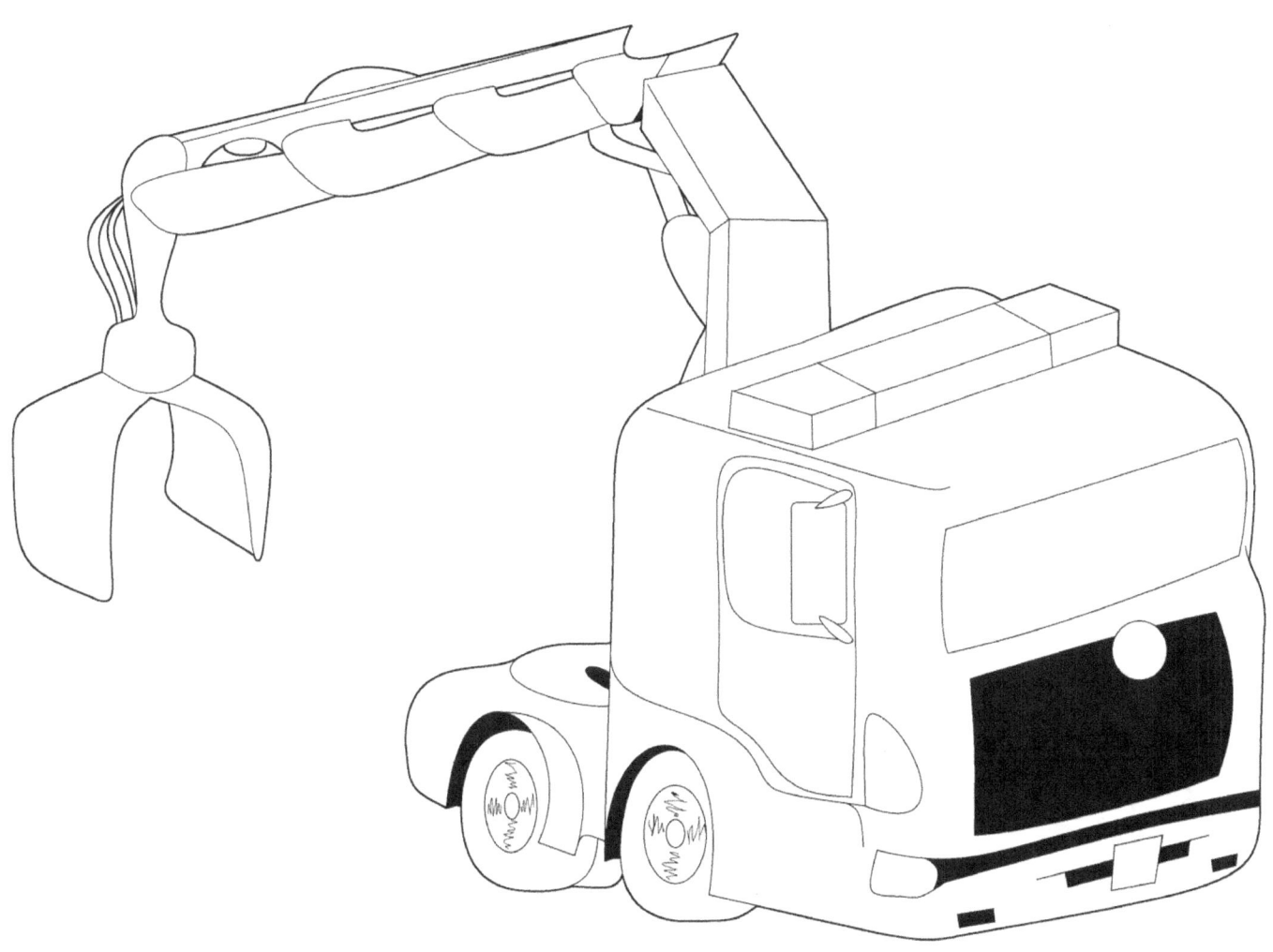

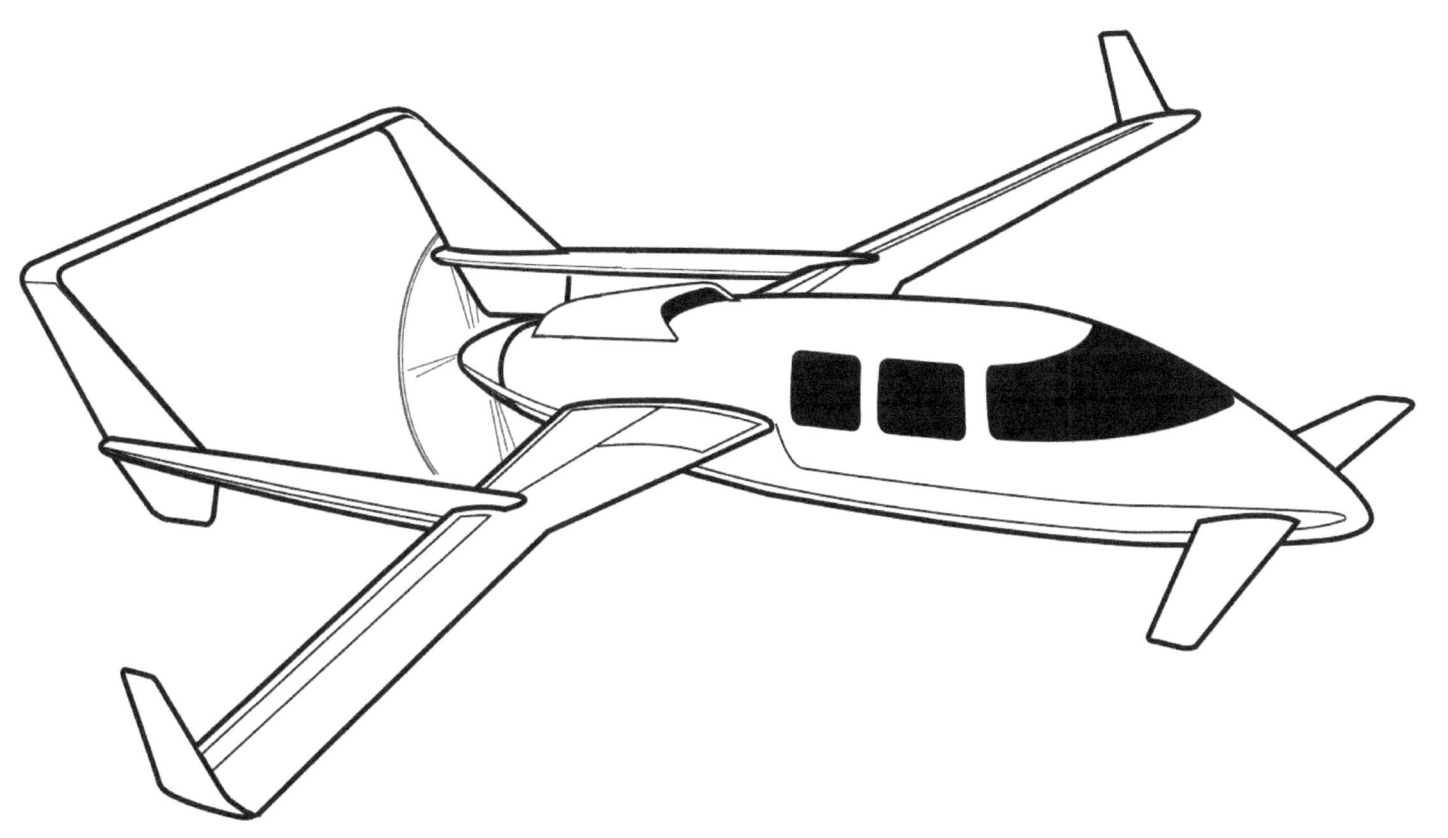

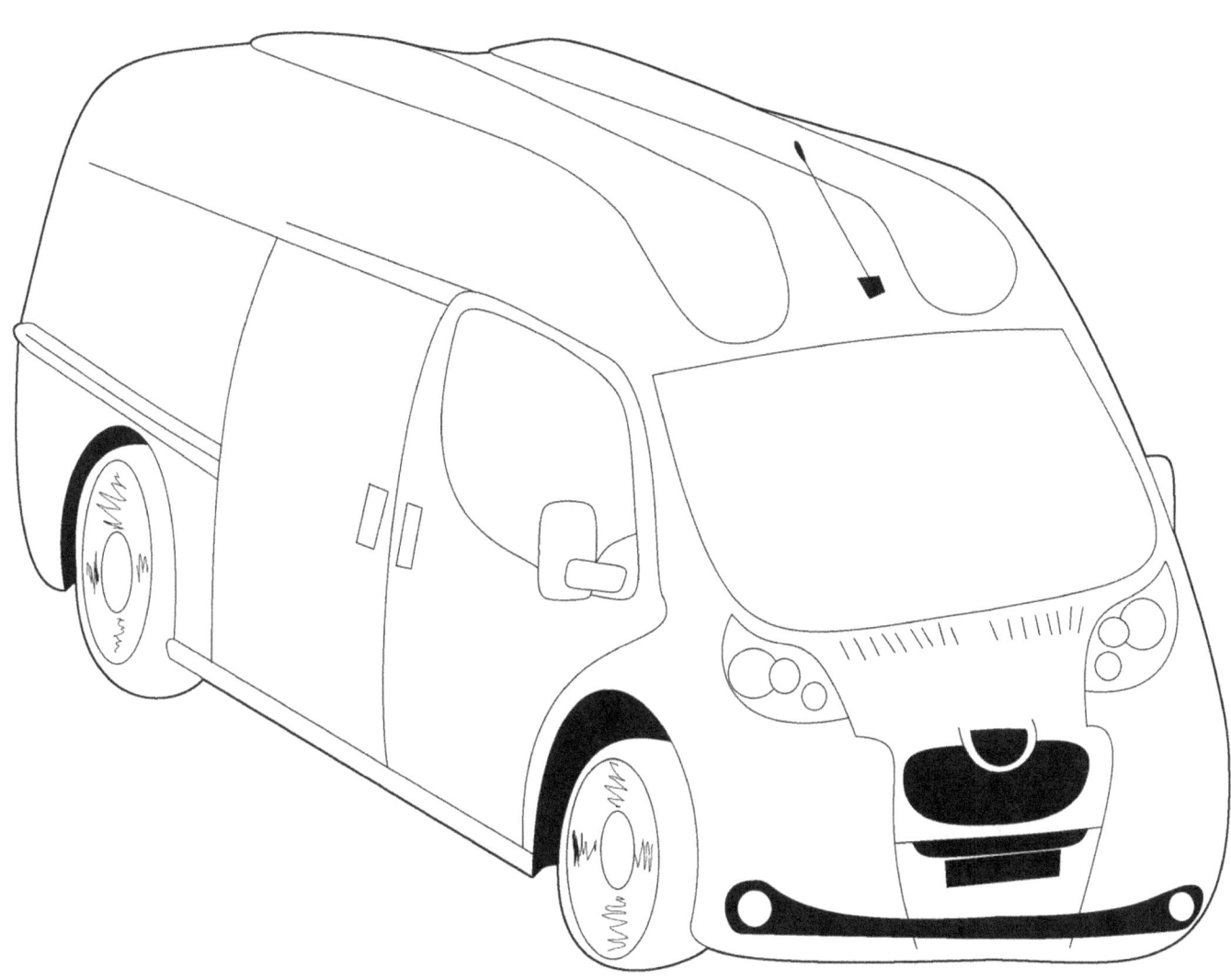

Conclusion

Thank you so much for purchasing this book. If you enjoyed it, then please leave an Amazon review. Reviews are the lifeblood for our publishing endeavors - Leaving a positive review would mean the world to us.

Cheers!
- Sunny Happy Kids